# Grieving for a Smoke

By Gary D. Strunk

**TEACH Services, Inc.**
PUBLISHING
*www.TEACHServices.com*

--------------------------------

Copyright © 2012 TEACH Services, Inc.
ISBN-13: 978-1-57258-797-7 (Paperback)
ISBN-13: 978-1-57258-798-4 (Hardback)
ISBN-13: 978-1-57258-799-1 (ePub)
ISBN-13: 978-1-57258-825-7 (Kindle/Mobi)

Library of Congress Control Number: 2012938576

Published by

**TEACH Services, Inc.**

P U B L I S H I N G

*www.TEACHServices.com*

# Table of Contents

*iii*

# Preface

I was on leave of absence from a doctoral program in nutrition at the University of Toronto when my stepfather passed away. A friend sent me a copy of the little book *Good Grief* by Granger Westberg. As I read about the stages of grief as Westberg described, I immediately recognized similar stages many ex-smokers experience after giving up smoking. I had helped hundreds of smokers stop smoking through the Five-Day Plan to Stop Smoking and 2-5-4 Smoke No More smoking cessation programs. And I had observed a pattern of suffering some smokers go through after giving up smoking.

As I dealt with my own grief over the death of my stepfather, I recognized the connection between quitting smoking and grieving, and the idea for this book was born. It was this realization that also caused me to change my doctoral studies from nutrition to "the grief response associated with smoking cessation" in the Community Health Division of the Faculty of Medicine at the University of Toronto.

At that time, 1982 and after, I read every book and journal article I could find on grieving. Since then a lot more research has been done, but the basics had already been recognized, mapped, and tested. *Grieving for a Smoke* is not a scientific treatise. Credits are not always given for the observations and ideas developed by the pioneers in this field— pioneers to whom we are all indebted—but a bibliography can be found at the end of this book that documents the many works I used for my research. I have deliberately tried to avoid psychobabble and too much scientific jargon in my writing. Once in a while no term fits as well as a technical term, but I try to define such terms.

I could write in the style of scientific articles, for example, "Lindesmith's concept that the 'hook' of addiction is '... fixed by negative rather than by positive reinforcement, by relief and avoidance of discomfort and pain rather than by positive pleasure' is reflected by Reinert who combines Wikler's idea of a cyclical polarity in addictive functioning with Lindesmith's thesis of the importance of craving to the maintenance of the addictive cycle" (Harrup 1979, 241).

Instead, I write, "An addict is hooked by

avoiding the discomfort of going without, and enjoying the rewards of indulging." Some books spend a lot of time and space describing and illustrating a concept. I could be criticized for writing too briefly, but I usually state it once and stop. That comes from a two-year discipline in my college days.

While a student at Oregon State College, I worked in a seed laboratory where basic research projects were conducted. The studies had implications for organizations worth millions, so they had enormous consequences. My task for two years was to take reams of data, tables, and graphs and boil them down into as few words and pages as possible. As a result, *Grieving for a Smoke* may be a smaller book than the topic deserves. But I like small books, and books that are easy to read. Additional material can be found in the appendices.

I have written this book in hopes that smokers will be able to put a label on the emotions they may go through when they entertain the idea of quitting and then again after they quit and sometimes have started again. The validity of my hypothesis that some smokers experience genuine grief over the cessation of smoking is borne by the firsthand interviews reported in this book and the responses I receive from smokers and ex-smokers in my audiences when I present the concepts described in this book. Addicted smokers identify with and affirm all that is within these pages.

Most smokers talk about missing cigarettes even when they say they hate them. They are not missing the cigarette as much as they are missing smoking the cigarette. They don't want to just look at cigarettes or hold them or admire them. They want to *smoke* them, because that's where the rewards are. Thus, in an effort to speak accurately, I should always use the word smoking, but that's not the way we talk. Therefore, sometimes when I should say smoking, I will say cigarettes because "cigarettes" is the way we talk. "He likes cigarettes." No, he doesn't; he likes smoking cigarettes. I'm not splitting hairs, but there is a *BIG* difference between liking cigarettes and liking smoking cigarettes, which I will address in chapter 2.

It is awkward to always write politically correct using gender-neutral terms such as person or individual, so I sometimes used he and sometimes she for convenience. But please note that what is written in this book applies to both sexes.

\* \* \* \* \* \* \*

# Chapter 1

# The Pilot Study

Grief is not a simple emotion of missing something. It's a complex collage of stages or phases grievers go through over a period of days, months, or even years. These stages have been mapped by early grief specialists so that they are quite predictable when there is a loss of some*one* dear or something dear, such as moving from a childhood home, the loss of a job, or, in this case, the loss of smoking; not the loss of cigarettes, but the loss of smoking. People often think they miss cigarettes. They don't. They miss smoking. There is a big difference, but I'll explain that later.

Some authors challenge the idea of predictable stages to grief because the stages don't always come in order, and some may be missing. In his well-documented book *The Other Side of Sadness*, George Bonanno takes issue with the idea of *stages*. Instead he emphasizes the *resilience* of most grieving persons and the great variations of people's responses to grief.

However, grief specialists have themselves recognized these variations to the degree that they say "variableness" is a characteristic of grief. Furthermore, throughout his book

---

## People often think they miss cigarettes. They don't. They miss smoking.

---

Bonanno refers to many emotions and behaviors of grief consistent with stages. Granger Westberg himself recognizes such variation:

> ...Every person does not necessarily go through all these stages, nor does a person necessarily go through them [his ten stages] in this order. Moreover, it is impossible to differentiate clearly between each of these stages, for a person never moves neatly from one stage to the other (1971, 20).

In appendix B I have listed various stages mapped by different early grief "mappers." While there are some variations in the lists, depending on the point of view of the mapper and the subjects being studied, there is a commonality in the stages that is immediately recognizable.

Grieving persons grieve. Sometimes grieving persons repress their grief; not in denial, but because they simply are not ready to deal with the overwhelming emotions their loss precipitates. They may come and go in waves, again and again, sometimes in a predictable order and sometimes not, some present, some missing, but nevertheless, most stages are there if a person is genuinely grieving. So I will, for the sake of some order and simplicity, describe grief as a variable series of stages of emotions and behaviors as they pertain to the smoker and ex-smoker.

One person on my doctoral committee had walked away from his smoking habit with relative ease, so he doubted that anyone missed smoking so severely as to be described as "grieving." So I was required to conduct a pilot study to justify my hypothesis that some smokers grieve over the loss of smoking. It didn't take long to establish in the minds of all who listened to my taped interviews that as many as 80 percent of the ex-smokers in the study were "grieving for a smoke," some severely.

The subjects for my pilot study were not individuals who had quit on their own, even though all had tried. They were a total of fifteen men and women who had stopped smoking six months earlier through a group cessation program conducted by the Canadian Cancer Society. Each person gave permission to be interviewed. After asking several routine questions such as how long had they smoked, what brands had they smoked, how many cigarettes a day had they smoked, and had they gone back to smoking (some had, others hadn't), I

---

## Grieving persons grieve. Sometimes grieving persons repress their grief.

---

came to a key question, "Do you miss cigarettes?" Or for those who had started smoking again, "Did you miss cigarettes?"

I had only two say rather gleefully, "Nope, not at all!" Both were young and had smoked for only a few years. One was a recreational smoker, smoking only on weekends. But the others! I cannot find words to express the mournful tones of some of the others as they groaned with a far away look in their eyes, "Oh yes... " They would usually add, "God, I miss cigarettes." Then came the next key question that I tenderly asked in this qualitative research-style survey, "How *much* do you miss cigarettes?" or "During the time you weren't smoking, how *much* did you miss cigarettes?" That is where their grief became apparent.

Mrs. Smith (alias), who seemed to be a

well-adjusted, professionally trained individual, active in civic affairs, confessed, "I hate to tell you this. I lost my mother two years ago, and we were close, and I missed her, and I still do, but I missed cigarettes a lot more than I did my mother. I suffered more over giving up cigarettes than I ever did over my mom's death."

Pointing to the couch, she said, "I would lie down on that couch with my hands folded over my chest, and I would lie there for two hours wondering if I could ever live without cigarettes, wanting to smoke, yearning to smoke, waiting for those dreadful feelings to pass." Her "yearnings" didn't pass in just a day or two. They went on for days, well beyond the chemical addiction of nicotine. She had been in a turbulent turmoil of grief. Six months after quitting, which is when I interviewed her, her feelings and behavior were typical of grief—pining, sighing, reminiscing, fearful of coping without cigarettes.

It was important not to introduce the word "grief" or "grieving" so as not to bias the results. If the word came up at all, it had to come from the participant. As I interviewed one man who had returned to smoking, and I asked him the key question, "How *much* did you miss cigarettes?", there came this mournful, depressed, haunting sound in his voice with an almost frightened stare in his eyes. "Oh yes! Yes, I missed them... dreadfully. The whole time I wasn't smoking, for three or four months, I felt... I felt... sad. Yes! That's the word, sad. I felt this terrible sadness. I longed for the... the whatever it was, to smoke again. Funny, I didn't particularly *like* cigarettes. At first I was glad I stopped smoking, like everyone else in the class. But soon, very soon, I felt this terrible sadness coming over me, like, like I was grieving for a friend who had died."

Mrs. Brown (alias) was in her office when I interviewed her, carrying on her work of counseling persons struggling with alcohol. Yes, she missed cigarettes. "How *much* do you miss cigarettes?" I queried. She stared at me quizzically as though I wasn't going to believe what she was about to tell me.

"How much do I miss cigarettes? How much do I miss cigarettes, you ask? Oh, I don't know if you can believe this. I don't know if you can understand this. But if you had a friend that you really loved, that you really, really, *really* loved, and that friend died, that's how much I miss cigarettes." Then she added wistfully with that deep mournful sigh and that far away look in her eyes, "I will always miss cigarettes."

I have to tell you, reader, that my heart went out to these people. At times I felt guilty as if I was using them for my benefit. My doctoral hypothesis rode on their answers. At the same time I felt quietly gleeful that my hypothesis was being affirmed. But to witness their sorrow, the hurt they were feeling, I could not help but be moved. At the same time, each of them seemed grateful that someone was asking, that someone cared and understood what they were going through. I immediately became their friend.

There were specific stages of grief they mentioned and dwelt on that will be covered in

---

## "Oh yes! Yes, I missed them... dreadfully. The whole time I wasn't smoking...."

---

chapter three, but for now their mournful answers to the question, "How *much* do you miss cigarettes," were enough to establish "grief."

A retired newspaper editor who after six months was still not smoking answered me with a far away look in his eyes as his voice trailed off longingly, "You know, there were only two cigarettes I really enjoyed. One was after we met the deadline in the afternoon. I would go into my office alone. I would push back my chair and light up a well-deserved cigarette. God, I miss that cigarette! And the other one was at night... after my wife had gone to bed.

I would lean back in my easy chair and in the quietness of my thoughts I would smoke my last cigarette of the day."

Tears were now in his eyes, and his voice quivered. My question triggered memories of his ceremonial smoking, the ones he enjoyed, and now didn't. My questions were painful to him; painful because of how much he missed certain smokes. Not really! It was how much he missed the pleasant memories those smokes had mediated to him. I will expound upon this in chapter two.

As I mentioned earlier, grief has many phases. One of them is anger. Several interviewees had either passed through their anger, were on their way to anger, or were stuck on anger. This can be kind of ironic. I have helped many people stop smoking. At first they are grateful for my help. But if I catch them at the wrong time later, they can be mad at me and everyone else for "taking cigarettes away from them." Nobody did that. They gave them up themselves. But anger can be irrational.

When I went to visit Mrs. Green (alias), she wasn't home yet, so I visited with her husband and son while we waited. Both of them said they wished she would go back to smoking. She had undergone such a personality change since she stopped smoking that they confessed, "We can't stand her anymore. She is miserable, and miserable to live with, just always mad. She lashes out at the least annoyance, and at the closest target of opportunity. She has become so mean; she is probably too mean to go back to smoking." They were serious when they said they wished she would go back to smoking because she was stuck in anger. It's important not to get stuck in any one stage but to keep moving forward.

---

## My questions were painful to him; painful because of how much he missed certain smokes.

---

It is difficult to convey in words the deep-seated sadness many of these persons were feeling, yet felt free enough to express it. It seemed a relief to them to share with someone who might understand their sense of loss. And these were just a sampling of many who had stopped smoking. Some of my colleagues who were conducting stop smoking programs at that time recognized immediately, when I put a name to it, that *grief* was what some of their patients were going through.

It is important to mention that not everyone grieves over no longer smoking. Some are free and happy. Some are able to stop smoking on their own, and they hardly give it a second thought. While others are victims of temptation for years to come, not understanding what was happening to them in their grief, nor having successfully gone through the grieving process.

My father-in-law was one who never handled his grief nor completely broke from cigarettes. He began smoking at age 13. At age 62 he stopped smoking. Then one day, thirteen years after he quit, a couple came to visit my in-laws for a few days. The woman was a smoker. She smoked around my father-in-law, which was hard on him. When they left, my father-in-law came into the house and asked his wife, "Do you think I should start smoking again?" Now what kind of a question is that? He didn't ask, "Would it be okay with you if I start smoking again?"

He was hoping for permission to once again have what he wanted and what he missed very much. After quitting thirteen years earlier, he was still yearning to smoke. Instead, he decided to eat Life Savers. He kept them in his shirt pocket where he used to keep his pack of cigarettes. Throughout the day he would reach into his pocket just like he would reach for a smoke and pull out a Life Saver. His face broke out from too much sugar. He died of lung cancer fifteen years after he stopped smoking.

\* \* \* \* \* \* \*

# Chapter 2

# Why a Smoker Smokes

## Understanding Addiction

The standard definition of addiction includes both a chemical component and a psychological component. The chemical component in smoking is nicotine, and the psychological component is the meaning and value of smoking to the smoker. Smoking is considered one of the hardest addictions to break. Why? And why would a person actually "grieve" over no longer smoking? It's not because of nicotine. While the pharmacological addiction to nicotine is essential for a short while, it plays a minor role in initially hooking the smoker and in luring the ex-smoker back to smoking compared to the psychological component with the meaning and value the smoker has invested in the cigarette. Let's take a look.

# The Chemical Component

The main chemical component in tobacco is nicotine, to which the body develops a tolerance. Building a tolerance means the brain becomes less and less responsive to a certain level of a drug so that more of the drug is needed to obtain the desired effect until the brain is satiated.

When the first bolus of nicotine hits the brain, a sense of alertness is felt. Noradrenalin, acetylcholine, and other brain nerve transmitters are released, preparing for fight or flight. Epinephrine (and nor-epinephrine) are released from the adrenal glands. The

---

## Smoking is considered one of the hardest addictions to break. Why?

---

heart beats faster. The liver releases glucose into the bloodstream for energy. Then as tolerance (deadness or numbness) builds, more and more nicotine is needed to obtain the desired effect. Nicotine also releases dopamine in the brain, giving the smoker a feeling of pleasure. Dopamine regulates hunger and thirst, creating a felt need for food and water, but for the addicted smoker, it calls for another cigarette. Cigarette smokers are generally slimmer when smoking than after they quit. While smoking, their hunger feeling was satisfied with a cigarette. After quitting, they eat.

An experienced smoker skillfully regulates the amount of stimulation and/or pleasure he or she receives by the number of cigarettes, the frequency of puffs, and the depth of inhalation. It's called "finger-tip control."

As the desired stimulation or feeling of comfort from the carefully controlled nicotine level falls between cigarettes, an irritating letdown sets in, known as withdrawal or "twitters," which the smoker interprets as a need for another cigarette.

The body does not store nicotine. It begins metabolizing or neutralizing the nicotine immediately so that withdrawal is felt within twenty to thirty minutes after the cigarette is smoked. Half the nicotine from one cigarette is metabolized in about two hours.

The person who smokes about one cigarette an hour or about a pack a day forms the following pattern of stimulation. This smoker is called a "peak seeker." Between cigarettes the nicotine level falls to a low level, then the next cigarette delivers a sharp jolt or peak to the brain.

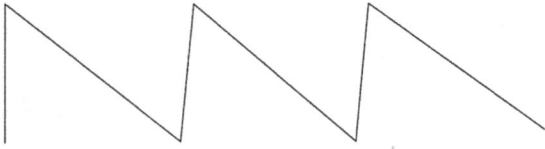

Chain smokers who smoke four or more cigarettes an hour produce the following pattern. These smokers are called, "high riders." The continual stimulation doesn't come down until an hour or two after the last cigarette of the day. By morning the nicotine is long gone from the system, and the first cigarette of the day can affect the smoker much like the very first cigarette ever smoked—cough, cough! The cough is not from the nicotine. It is from the smoke, which contains tars and toxic chemicals that make the lungs go into spasms and paralyzes the cilia lining the trachea.

After a smoker has completely—emphasis on completely—stopped smoking for three or four days, the irritated receptors in the brain and body settle down. Very quickly the *chemically*-generated twitters are gone. Chemical withdrawal is past. That doesn't mean that craving is past, but the cause of the cravings are more psychological than chemical. These statements contrast sharply with the idea that nicotine is the major culprit in smoking addiction. But is it nicotine? If nicotine were the pri-

---

## The body does not store nicotine. It begins metabolizing or neutralizing the nicotine immediately.

---

mary problem, then give the smoker nicotine, and he should no longer want to smoke. But unfortunately they still want to smoke even while using nicotine aids. It's worth noting that people don't become addicted to nicotine by chewing nicotine gum or using nicotine patches or inhaling nicotine puffers? That's why these aids can be helpful in getting smokers off of smoking, but not by themselves because people are addicted to smoking more than to nicotine.

Why will smokers go back to smoking, especially two or ten years after they quit? Not because of the chemical component, even though the ex-smoker's brain is permanently wired for smoking. She goes back because of the psychological component. The chemical component of addiction is essential and powerful for awhile, but it plays a surprisingly minor role compared to the psychological component, which is far more powerful and enduring. Therefore, trying to cure smoking by only addressing the felt need for nicotine fails to address the larger and stronger portion of addiction. So let's examine the psychological component.

# The Psychological Component

The psychological component of any addiction is a powerful reason why it is so difficult for most to walk away from the addiction. The psychological component of addiction says that in order to be addicted a person must believe that nothing else can do for him what the object of his addiction can do. This object provides him comfort and pleasure in the form of fulfillment, reward, and/or stimulation (positive affect). It also provides him relief or escape from danger, unhappiness, and various stresses (negative affect).

In general we can say that the smoking habit is highly invested with meaning and value, perhaps the most invested bad habit in the human race. Smoking can mean more to smokers than their children, more than their spouses, more than their jobs, and more than a leg or a lung, or their life. Here is how smoking becomes so meaningful.

1. **Grown-up Behavior**—Teenagers view smoking as adult behavior, so the sooner they can smoke, the sooner they will be considered an adult. They will be all grown-up with no one telling them what to do. They will be in control.

    At the same time, smoking is used as a means of defying adult authority, especially if adults have told them not to smoke. Smoking means liberation and independence from adult control.

    So, on one hand, children smoke because they want to be like grown-ups. On the other hand, they smoke because they want to be free from grown-up control. Smoking now means more than puffing on dried weeds rolled in paper. Most kids don't even like the taste or the effects of smoking to begin with. Nevertheless, in spite of the discomfort, they aspire to smoke because smoking affirms their maturity and independence. And here's the tricky part. Smoking continues to affirm and re-affirm their maturity and their independence even into their adult years.

**2. Role Modeling**—No young person decides to roll some dried leaves into paper, set it on fire, and breathe in the smoke without ever seeing someone else do it. Young people see special people smoke. So young people and adults are led to believe that smoking is a part of the successful image. Cigarette advertisers have portrayed smoking as glamorous by linking it with screen stars, sports figures, happy campers, and handsome, virile cowboys.

By 1991, 70 percent of the first-time smokers started with Marlboro. To smoke is to be handsome and successful. So much so that kids practice in front of the mirror how to hold a cigarette and how to blow out the smoke artistically or casually as if they were long-time smokers, all of which takes practice to look cool. Guys practice how to hold their elbows to look tough or suave. And in the years to come, the image of these role models or the hologram of their own self-image still propels the smoking habit from deep within the covert shadows of the mind.

We should include here the influence

of a young person's peers. If their friends are smoking and this young person wants the approval and acceptance of his or her friends, they will... You can fill in the blank.

3. **Memories of Happiness**—Smoking is associated with happy times. Smoking is used for celebration and relaxation. After completing a hard task or signing a contract, smokers reward themselves with a cigarette. Following a meal, smokers push back and relax with a cigarette. When strangers meet, if they are smokers they offer each other a cigarette. Friends share friendship by sharing a cigarette. Smoking means celebration, hospitality, happiness, and bonds of friendship.

In time, smoking carries with it a flood of happy memories mediated *by a thousand repeated events of "happiness."* Because of these pleasant memories, a smoker can find pleasure or companionship in smoking a cigarette even in times of loneliness. A cigarette is the smoker's closest friend, closer than a brother, in his pocket close to his heart.

TO MY CIGARETTE: You are closer to me than any living creature, reposing in my pocket near my heart. With my lips I caress you more than I do my family. When I awake my thoughts turn to you and remain there all day. I worship at your shrine with burnt offerings constantly. At my desk the fires seldom go out on your altar. I scatter your incense of smoke in the faces of women and children. I call upon you for help more than I call upon my Creator. I pay more money for you than I pay to the church and charities combined. I risk my life for you. By smoking I take one chance in eight of having lung cancer and twice as many chances of death from heart attack. I take no such risks for my religion. I bear in my body the marks of my devotion to you: the color of my fingertips and skin. My body is so soaked with tar incense that when I perspire many people hold their noses and walk away. A new light is dawning, I have become your slave. I do not smoke, but I suck one end of the cigarette while you smoke at the other. I am a sucker"

(Author Unknown, *Life and Health Magazine South Africa,* vol. 6, no. 6, 1975).

4. **Neuromuscular Ritual**—Couple all the pleasant memories (cognitions) with the neurophysiology of a habit—the neuromuscular ritual of reaching for a cigarette, tapping it, putting it in the mouth, lighting it without getting smoke in his/her eyes, then inhaling the first drag and blowing out the smoke artistically or casually, and relaxing—and you have a ritual that is hard to let go of. For "handlers," it is something to do with their hands, but only *after* they become dependent on cigarettes. But there's more! Handling affects the mind, for the will follows the work of the hands so that the desire and will to smoke is supported by the very act of smoking. Positive feedback! Vicious cycle!

This neuromuscular ritual is associated with every waking activity. A typical smoker smokes a cigarette upon rising, another while listening to the morning news, and another after breakfast or instead of breakfast. He lights up again on the way to work. The following does not now apply in some states. After he gets to work and gets organized, he may smoke another to get started, or one to get organized. Redundancy noted! Later there is a coffee hour or smoke break or restroom stop. Even a conversation with a friend in the office or on the phone may call for a cigarette. And if a contract is signed, a cigarette is used to celebrate the event. And of course there is a cigarette after lunch and three or four more in the afternoon. Driving home at the close of the day calls for another cigarette. As well as one after supper while sitting in front of the TV or reading the newspaper or playing cards with friends. And finally one last cigarette is enjoyed just before bedtime.

Each time the smoker reaches for a cigarette, pulls it out, taps it, puts it in his mouth, lights up, inhales, and then blows the smoke artistically or casually out, he relaxes. He's done it thousands of times. The movements are done without thinking. It's now an automatic reflex. But when the cigarette is no longer there, he keeps reaching again and again, and he feels a little irritated, "A part of me is missing, and I want it back."

Nearly every waking activity is a cue to smoke. A smoker interacts *meaningfully* with a cigarette more times a day than he does with his spouse. He thinks about cigarettes more than he thinks about his children. Only two or three are really enjoyed. The rest are either tolerated or smoked in pursuit of the same pleasure that the two or three brought.

5. **Smoking helps**—Most importantly the smoker believes that smoking helps. Even when he has heard that cigarettes are bad for his health, he believes smoking helps him. And nothing else can do for him what smoking does for him. Trying to persuade him otherwise is like asking him to deny truth because smoking does help.

For example:

a. Smoking calms the experienced smoker. When a smoker is upset she will reach for a cigarette and immediately experience a calming effect, even before she smokes it. I witnessed an example of reaching for a cigarette by a smoker that was both comical and pitiful. I was talking to a friend in Palmer, Alaska, when the 1963 9.2 Alaskan earthquake hit. A woman came running out of the store where everything was falling off the shelves and ran up to us. Her face was white with fright. She was trembling. She opened her purse and fumbled for a cigarette. Finally she grabbed one and stuck it in her mouth, but she put the wrong end in. She swore, threw it to the ground, and grabbed another, which she finally got lit. Only then did she begin to settle down.

The dopamine kicked in. That helped. But smoking by itself with all its acquired psychological rewards helped! While dopamine brings pleasure, nicotine also stimulates the nerves, and the lack of nicotine in the withdrawal phase creates nervousness. Then the act of smoking temporarily relieves their nervousness. They have experienced it hundreds of times. Are they wrong? No, they are right. But is it the cigarette, or is it the highly invested act of smoking that calms them... for the moment?

At one time medics were taught to give a wounded soldier a lighted cigarette, unless of course he had a sucking chest wound. As soon as the wounded smoker took a drag, he calmed down. He believed, "I'm OK. I'm going to live." Smoking could prevent the victim from going into shock. The smoker had performed this meaningful ritual so many times that even though injured in combat, he relaxed. It was more powerful than an infant sucking his thumb when he is upset. It was not the nicotine. It was not the tobacco. He could get the same effect from a lettuce cigarette.

It was the calming effect of the neuromuscular ritual, plus years of coming of age, of liberation, of cele-bration, of reward for a job well done, of friendship, of happiness. All he needed to do was light up a cigarette and peace, to some extent, pervaded.

It is important to note that this did not help an injured soldier who was a non-smoker, only the smoker.

**b.** Another reason the smoker believes that nothing helps like smoking is that cigarettes pick the smoker up when he feels down. In seven seconds nicotine acts on the brain. The nervous system is stimulated. The pupils dilate, the heart beats faster, peripheral vessels constrict, blood pulls back from the skin, adrenalin (epinephrine) is released, and the liver releases sugar into the bloodstream that gives added energy. Smoking gives him a "lift." It truly does.

When the smoker comes to believe that a cigarette will help, and only a cigarette will help, then the psychological trap is sprung. He is addicted. And to a large extent his thinking is correct. Nothing acts quite like a cigarette.

If a heroin addict is confined to jail for nine months, his chemical receptors in the brain and, therefore, his chemical addiction for heroine is long past. Is he still an addict? Absolutely! Once released and facing his first crisis, he will seek out heroine because he still *believes* that heroine, and only heroine, can relieve his distress. His boutons are fixed from many repeated events. The addict has permanently altered his central nervous system. That's why a smoker can return to smoking 10 years later without any relearning.

To become addicted, a person must believe she is helped by the substance she is taking and that nothing else can help like that substance. If a patient experiences pain and is then told that she will be given morphine to relieve her pain, and she experiences relief from her

---

## To become addicted, a person must believe she is helped by the substance she is taking.

---

pain, she may become addicted to morphine. If however she is given morphine without her knowing it so that she is not allowed to feel pain or allowed to sense relief from pain, she will not likely become addicted to morphine.

There are other theories of addiction, but if I were to present them all, this would no longer be a small book. What I have written above is the heart of the psychological addiction of smoking. I have cited enough for the reader to see how a smoking addiction is formed and why the psychological component of that addiction is so powerful and enduring.

And even if I were to write what I thought

was an exhaustive presentation of addiction theory and grief theory, I'm convinced that some old timer would come up to me and say, "I got one more fer yer."

## "Addicted" to Pleasure

As a point of interest, since food, sex, gambling, or the rush of excitement have no chemical substance to which the body builds a tolerance, are these really addictions according to the standard definition of addiction? No, but there is a similarity in that all of these behaviors tickle the pleasure center through the internal chemistry of the brain, that is, if we consider them pleasurable.

The hypothalamus, which houses the pleasure center, is in the floor of the brain. Whenever an activity is perceived as pleasurable, a tiny electrical impulse is felt in the hypothalamus, thus signaling enjoyment, and we want to enjoy again.

In experiments with monkeys, electrical probes are inserted into the hypothalamus. Each time a tiny electrical impulse is delivered to the hypothalamus, the monkey feels pleasure. Next, the electrode is connected (wireless today) to a bar or trigger in the monkey's cage which when pressed by the monkey will send an electrical impulse to his brain. At some point the monkey accidentally presses the bar and receives this good feeling. Soon he learns that it is only in this area of the cage that he receives this good feeling. Then, after a few more accidental pressings, he *learns* that each time he presses this bar he receives a wonderful feeling, so now he presses it deliberately. Pretty soon he will sit there and press the bar again and again as fast as his little fingers will press because if feels sooooo good!

If something upsets him, he will run quickly and press the bar. Now he feels better. Put food in front of him, and even though he is hungry he may press the bar to feel better, thus growing thin. The female may even deny her maternal instincts to care for her infant. If the lab worker makes threatening gestures at her infant rather than protecting it, she will run over and press the bar. She will exchange responsible, constructive behavior for a pleasant feeling. Addicts are "pressing the bar."

The psychological trap has sprung. The smoker has invested so much value in becoming of age through smoking; in looking like and acting like her role models; in using cigarettes for celebration, hospitality, and friendship; and in training his body to reach, to tap, to light up, to inhale and exhale, and to believe that "If I only had a cigarette, and only a cigarette will do, life would be better." A twenty-year smoker at only one pack a day has rewarded himself with that *meaningful* habit 146,000 times. Nothing can take the place of smoking. No wonder smokers who quit smoking miss cigarettes enough to grieve over their loss.

* * * * * * *

# Chapter 3

# **Grieving for a Smoke**

The Department of Health and Human Services has identified six categories of smokers by what they get out of smoking: stimulation, handling, pleasurable relaxation, crutch (tension reduction), craving (psychological addiction), habit. I have found that all of these categories of smokers can experience grief at varying levels depending on how significant smoking was to them for whatever they got out of smoking.

To the average reader, the term "grief" may convey a rather naïve meaning of "a deep and poignant distress caused by or as if by bereavement" (Webster 1973). But to appreciate the dynamics of grief it must be defined through its experiential components. Schroeder, citing the work of several others, offers the following summary:

Grief is defined as a series of emotional responses that follow the perception or anticipation of a loss of one or more valued or significant objects. The ability to experience grief for any such loss is gradually formed in the course of normal development. Grief is more than a symptom of an ailment. It is the active involvement of the structure of values of the individual in a major situational experience. The response of grief can result from the loss of valued objects, such as a loved person, a cherished possession, a job, a status, a home, a country, an ideal, a part of the body. Grief runs a constant course, modified mainly by the abruptness of the loss, the nature of the preparation for the loss, and the significance of the lost object to the bereaved person (Hall 1974, 159).

The suggestion that grief is a response to smoking cessation comes as a surprise to some because to them grief connotes heartbroken shock with severe and somewhat indescribable emotional pain usually associated with the death of a loved one.

But grief is experienced in a wide range of emotional feelings from one person to another, from one situation to another, and from one form of loss to another. Perhaps more importantly, grief is characterized by a number of emotional, attitudinal, and behavioral components. When these component behaviors, feeling states, and mental states are present, grief

---

## Grief is defined as a series of emotional responses that follow the perception or anticipation of a loss.

---

is in process. These components are not separate and discrete entities. They form a fused, overlapping, interchanging collage that must be teased apart by probing questions.

Do smokers experience grief when quitting? Some have. Nurses Elaine Richard and Ann Shepard stopped smoking independently from each other (Richard and Shepard 1981). Elaine, acquainted with grief from having previously undergone a loss because of a divorce, "suddenly realized" in her fourth week of abstinence from cigarettes that she "was experiencing a grief reaction associated with the loss of a special friend—my cigarette!" (Ibid., 755).

After understanding the "theoretical basis" for her behavior, she was able "to accept it and to begin to develop coping strategies" (Ibid.).

Ann reported that "the loss of cigarettes was as acute as losing a friend. The feelings connected with the loss did not become evident until three to four months after I stopped smoking. At that time I experienced a sense of sadness, although my personal and professional lives were stable and pleasurable. The only changes in my life was not smoking" (Ibid., 756).

They then describe an application of loss theory to the emotional stages accompanying smoking cessation. They observed that "in smoking cessation, both grief from anticipation of loss and sadness from the actual loss are experienced" (Ibid.).

"When exploring our feelings, we identified a definite emptiness, which each of us described separately as 'like losing a good friend.' Initially this loss was experienced numerous times during the day with each craving for a cigarette.

"Both of us felt a sense of acceptance of our losses about 6-12 months after cessation. There was a conscious awareness of an end to a life-style that included smoking and a resolution of grief over a profound loss" (Ibid., 757).

Knowing that the stages of grief do not always follow in a neat, orderly fashion, I shall nevertheless discuss them as if in a sequence as I compare responses to the loss of smoking with the loss of a significant other.

As I describe the emotional levels in the following stages, some may sound like an exaggeration. But I am describing a composite individual made up of several different smokers. I have met smokers who have manifested all the symptoms described herein who have surprised me with the extreme level of grief they were suffering. That's what led me to write this book in hopes that these experiences might help someone cope with their own unexpected feelings. The signs of grief are as follows:

# Shock

Shock is often the first response to the news of some special person having been killed or seriously injured. Shock includes disbelief. "I don't believe it. How can that be? I just talked to him two hours ago." A person's mind may reel from the shock of the news. A whole nation reeled in shock at the death of President John F. Kennedy. Some who had never met the president wept uncontrollably.

When I learned of the loss of the crew of Challenger II, I watched the news clip again and again, hoping to see what others had failed to see, the crew escaping somehow. I personally saw the spacecraft Voyager II streak over the California desert minutes before it disintegrated over the Southeastern U.S. Disbelief is followed by a kind of emotional numbness or disorientation as a person's world begins to change.

We can experience shock over the news

---

## "When exploring our feelings, we identified a definite emptiness, which each of us described separately...."

---

of our own impending death when we learn that we have terminal cancer with only three months to live. That's shocking. Lung cancer from smoking can be devastating. It takes an average of eight years for the lump to grow dense enough to show on an X-ray, which leaves the victim an average of eight months to live. We may then go through many stages of grief before death. Elisabeth Kübler-Ross called this anticipatory grief.

So how can "shock" apply to quitting smoking? Let's say a smoker who has smoked for twenty or thirty years begins to toy with the idea of quitting. His psyche can actually reel at the thought of living without cigarettes. He doesn't even want to think about it. His whole world would change. The very thought of quitting can be so threatening, so "shocking," that he refuses to entertain the thought and instead puts it out of his mind for now. Going smokeless is so intimidating that he can only flirt with the idea of quitting, sometimes for years, before he summons enough courage to face the real possibility of going without.

I have listened to scores of testimonies of persons coming to my stop smoking programs. Some have reported numbness from the thought of quitting, with its disorienting sense of unreality surging through them as they contemplate the idea of quitting. Anticipating the death of their closest friend, a cigarette, throws them into anticipatory grief. After all, they have relied on cigarettes to supply their needs a thousand times—to calm them down, to diminish hunger, to bring them comfort, to give them companionship.

John Tamerin (1972) reported on a group of sixteen upper-middle class, well-educated, suburban housewives who experienced smoking cessation together. They expressed fears anticipatory to cessation based on their past experiences intimately associated with their individual efforts to quit smoking. They were fearful of being "unable to concentrate, organize thoughts, remember, drive a car, focus on housework, or even write a letter" (590).

Although their actual experience accompanying cessation was not as serious as they had anticipated, nevertheless, subjects reported lapses in concentration, problems remembering things, occasional difficulty driving, and, in some instances, a definitely altered threshold to the effects of alcohol so that amnesic episodes

---

## Shock is often the response to the news of some special person having been killed or seriously injured.

---

(blackouts) were reported following ingestion of small amounts of alcohol.

It should be noted that the experiences they reported were while they were quitting. They do not show how they may have grieved later on. I cite this case only to show that people do experience anticipatory grief. In some cases people actually tremble at the thought of quitting. Which brings us to stage two.

# Panic

Panic can follow shock. "How can I face life without Jane? For fifty years we have lived and loved and laughed together as constant companions." In like manner, "For thirty, forty, or fifty years cigarettes have been my companion, carried in my shirt pocket close to my heart." The thought of living without them can bring waves of terror. The dread of going through withdrawal! And just "living without them fills me with emptiness." Paradox noted! Yes, I've heard all these extreme words describing their fears.

The same panic felt in anticipation of quitting has hit many a smoker the day after quitting, and the day after that, and the day after that. Cigarettes have been their great stabilizer. Whenever something upset them, they reached for a cigarette, but now there is no cigarette. "I sat down in a panic, stunned over what to do with my hands and my shakes," one individual told me. Sometimes fleetingly, sometimes grippingly, panic comes and goes until the smoker finally grasps the truth that there is life after smoking.

Perhaps disorganization doesn't come under panic, but many smokers face disorganization and disorientation when they begin to quit. They have trouble concentrating. They have trouble getting started and following their usual routine without cigarettes. Much to their surprise, they realize that their lives have been ordered and organized around smoking.

## Physical Symptoms

If you were to see your 2-year-old son fall from a high railing and watch as his head hit the terrazzo floor, his lifeless body lying there in a heap, you would almost die inside. For days afterward, you might feel pain in your own body, stiffness in your joints and muscles, a lack of energy, and sleeplessness. A torrent of negative hormones came cascading out of the brain the moment you saw your son fall, merely from what you saw. No one laid a hand on you, yet you feel debilitating pain, loss of appetite, and only with difficulty can you put one foot in front of the other. What happened in your brain affected your whole body.

The grieving smoker does not experience

---

## "I sat down in a panic, stunned over what to do with my hands and my shakes"

---

physical symptoms as sharply as one who sees a loved one killed in front of him. It's more like watching a loved one die a slow death in a hospital bed, giving the watcher time to prepare. And yet the mixed emotions of relief and grief that come when someone finally dies still takes its toll on mind and body. The abstaining addict often appears to be a hypochondriac, complaining of a variety of illnesses, pains, and discomforts that he argues did not bother him when he was on the drug, because he could banish them at once with a fix.

The daily guide booklet used in the Five-Day Plan to Stop Smoking has a list of twenty-four symptoms to be checked off each day by the abstaining smoker, such as pain in the eyes, sleepiness, nausea, dizziness, and twelve different kinds and locations of headaches. Peoples' responses differed. Some couldn't sleep. Others could do nothing but sleep. Some had headaches. Some had stomachaches. The ironic thing is that we found that if we tore out that page and never let the smokers see the list, they suffered far fewer ill effects than if they saw it.

## Rumination

There is a time when all a grieving person can think about is the person who just died, or that lost puppy, or in this case cigarettes. "All I could think about was cigarettes. I thought I would go crazy if I didn't have one. Every time I turned around I thought about cigarettes. I tried to put them out of my mind, but it was like trying not to think of pink elephants," said one ex-smoker. Rumination can drive a person nuts. Cigarettes have been a part of his every waking activity. Now every waking activity reminds him of cigarettes.

Shortly after quitting, rumination can drive

a person right back to smoking. As one person shared with me, "If life without cigarettes is going to be like this, I can't stand it." But time heals, and in time most people stop thinking about cigarettes, or at least, cigarettes no longer dominate one's thinking. But when we remember that twenty to forty times a day for 365 days a year for the last thirty or forty years the smoker has reached for a cigarette and spent twenty minutes with it, why wouldn't he think about cigarettes, which leads to the next step.

## **Searching**

One of the benefits of going through a wake and a funeral or memorial service, and even the burial, is to affirm to our own consciousness that that person is dead and gone, no longer to be a companion. But the acceptance of that reality can be very slow in coming. If John used to come home every day at 5:30 p.m. and drive into the driveway, get out of his car, and walk up the steps to the back porch, then every day at 5:30 p.m., long after the funeral, his wife's brain triggers this thought, "I think I hear his car driving up now," as she waits for his footsteps and the opening of the screen door.

"Searching" can be *much* worse in cases of

divorce or a breakup than it is for a person who has lost someone to death. That person you love is still out there, and you see her from the back a few aisles over in the store. It's her hair. You are sure it's her. Slowly, no, quickly you walk around the aisles to catch a glimpse of her face. Your heart beats faster. It's her; you know it. But when you see her face, it's not her. In bitter disappointment you grieve some more. You watch for her in all the familiar places, constantly searching, hoping to see her. You experience the heartbreak again and again.

The ex-smoker searches. She pulls open the drawer and reaches way back inside where she has always kept a carton of cigarettes. Yeah, she knows. She remembers throwing them out. Nevertheless, she looks again just in case there might be one. She opens the cup-

---

## "Searching" can be much worse in cases of divorce or a breakup.

---

board door and climbs up on a stool to see if maybe there is one left somewhere.

She drives by the store where she always bought her cigarettes. She peers inside, wondering if they still sell cigarettes in there. She watches others light up and take a drag, wanting to bum one off them. She reaches in her

purse. Nothing! She opens the glove compart-
ment of the car. Nothing! "There's got to be a
cigarette someplace. I'm not going to smoke it.
I just want to hold it for awhile, just a little
while." Uh-huh! She is searching, searching,
searching.

# Idealization

Here is the tricky one. It's as if God built into
us the ability to forget the bad and remember
only the good. In a very short time after a son is
killed in war or a spouse dies, the survivor remembers only the good and banishes the bad.

My mother and stepfather fought continually. Time after time he would stomp out of the
house or she would leave the room in a huff,
eyes throwing darts. Then, somehow in a few
hours they would get back together again. This
went on routinely for thirty years. Then within
three months after the death of my stepfather,
I heard my mother say, "One of the things I always treasured about him was that we never
fought." I smiled weakly but sympathetically as
I heard her "idealize."

Idealization can lead a smoker right back
to smoking. Soon he cannot remember all the
many, many reasons he gave up smoking—his
coughing, his chest pain, the threat of cancer,
the price of cigarettes, his children begging

him to quit, the great waste of time, the loss of control. Control! Cigarettes had controlled his life. Yes, they dictated where he would sit in the movie so he could get out in case he needed a nicotine fix. Cigarettes chose his friends for him and dictated where he would sit in the restaurant. Cigarettes controlled his life. He hated them. No, he loved them. The dissonance of ambivalence is schizophrenic.

But now he can only remember the good. "You know, I really enjoyed smoking. Yes, that's it. I was one of those who enjoyed smoking. Smoking did a lot for me. I used to smoke with the guys... together. We really enjoyed each other's company. Cigarettes helped me. Why, when I needed something to calm me down, cigarettes would do the trick. They were something I could count on. I think some people are helped greatly by smoking; in fact, maybe I'd live longer if I smoked rather than if I didn't." Hmmmm!

Now that he's missing out on all those joys of smoking, whether he can articulate them or not, the next stage is pining.

# Pining

Now comes the sadness, the longing, the yearning to have again what she loved and treasured for so many years. With pining

53

comes deep sighing, sobbing-breathing, and "darkness." It's important to get past this stage as quickly as possible. There is nothing wrong with pining, yearning, missing, longing, or feeling sad for the loss of something dear. The danger is in determining to wear black the rest of one's life, of getting locked into any one phase rather than moving through to freedom.

However, sometimes it is comforting to feel the sadness of pining. After all, we miss them so terribly that we want to cry. It feels good to cry. It's okay to cry. There may even be some indulged self-pity. That's okay too, for awhile. Furthermore, our sorrow may be an indication of how much we loved that person, and how much he or she meant to us that we should feel so badly. In fact, it might seem wrong if we didn't grieve. "How can some people adjust to loss with a shrug of the shoulders? How can they just walk away? Didn't they care?"

That is what some may think. But always remember; everyone is different. Some have processed their grief well in advance through anticipatory grief. There are people who have come close to losing their spouses through illnesses who, in order to protect their own emotional health, have gone through certain stages of grief in advance so that they adjusted to the loss by distancing themselves from their spouses as a self-protective measure. I was an Army

chaplain during the Vietnam conflict, and I witnessed what some may call this strange phenomenon. It's not so strange. We often build
shells around ourselves to protect us from hurt.
I built my own shell during my year in Vietnam.

Now, can a person really pine over a cigarette, or technically over a smoke? Absolutely!

---

## It's important to get past this stage as quickly as possible. There is nothing wrong with pining.

---

The psychological component of smoking can
be so powerful that to face life without smoking brings great fear and a great sense of loss
with all of its accompanying sadness and sighing. In one case, Judy reported, "I couldn't
stop crying. I was so depressed. The light of
my life was gone. I know it sounds silly, but
oh, how I missed cigarettes." It's not the physical cigarettes of weeds and paper they missed
so much, even if they were "handlers," as it
is the semi-subliminal flood of memories each
cigarette brought of coming of age, of being
like their glamorous heroes, of companionship, of celebration. Cigarettes are highly invested with meaning, and when that's gone,
sadness follows.

Some smokers have lost a leg either by

injury or through diabetes and have grieved more over the loss of cigarettes than they have over the loss of their leg. Why? Because they had taken their legs for granted. They hadn't thought about their legs, but they had thought repeatedly about cigarettes again and again every time they "felt the need" for another smoke. So now their sadness may deepen into depression.

# Depression

With this stage, nothing seems interesting. Life is boring. "Every time I used to get on the phone, I lit up. Now I don't even want to call anyone. It's dullsville." The usual activities of cooking, doing dishes, or housework are no longer enjoyed, and nothing seems to break the monotony of living, especially when coupled with this pervasive sadness and sighing. That's depression.

Some people only want to sleep. Others can't sleep. They feel tired. They can't concentrate. Depression can be an awful thing. Clinical depression is usually more generalized, more global. They're just down. But the depression I'm describing here is a part of grief because the person believes that the specific thing he misses, a cigarette, and only a cigarette, will lift him out of his depression. But this kind of depression should pass if a person keeps doing his daily routine and doesn't permit others to wait on him.

Dr. Linda Ferry at the Veteran's Hospital in Loma Linda, California, has been very successful at helping smokers quit smoking by administering medications for depression. Heavy smokers have so benumbed their do-

---

## Some smokers have lost a leg ... and have grieved more over the loss of cigarettes.

---

pamine receptors that without their realizing it they are depressed as a result of smoking. Treating the depression along with other medications at the right time enables them to kick the habit.

Yet there are a few ex-smokers who never seem to be as happy as they were when they were smoking. But most usually don't get locked into depression if they busy themselves doing something. One man, as soon as he stopped smoking, started cutting pop cans into delicate figurines, rocking chairs, and statues. I have one on my shelf. He used to do that, years ago, that is, before he took up smoking. Once he started smoking, all his crafts went begging, until he quit smoking. Then for some reason he felt like doing them again. Initiative returned.

One woman returned to her delicate crocheting and knitting, the kind she used to do before she started smoking. Smoking had interfered with the more constructive use of her time and hands until she seemed content to just sit and smoke... and smoke, accomplishing nothing but smoking.

One university professor smoked his pipe while giving his lectures, which were timed to fifty minutes. During the summer he stopped smoking. The next year he completed each of the same lectures in thirty-five to forty minutes. Only then did he realize how much, ten to fifteen minutes, of his students' precious time he had spent fiddling with his pipe, tapping it, poking it, and just messing with it.

## Anger

Anger and resentment can lie just below the surface of different stages. Example: The ex-smoker who is instinctively "searching," who is disappointed at not finding a cigarette, can get angry at not finding one even though she stopped smoking by her own good sense. Anger can lie just below depression, feeling depressed because they can't smoke, then angry because they are depressed, and then angry at themselves for missing something as silly as injurious cigarettes. But they say anger is a good sign. It means that the person is accepting the reality that the missing object is gone.

Anger can come early in grief. My friend's wife suffered from bipolar disorder and subsequently threw herself under a train. At the news of her death, my friend's first response was shock, disbelief, then anger; no, not anger, rage. On his way from the morgue where he had to identify his wife, he hit the steering wheel so hard he expected to break it. He wasn't angry at her. He wasn't angry at God. He was just angry, angry that it happened.

Some people have actually been angry at their spouse for having died and leaving them alone. We mustn't take too seriously what people say or do in their anger when it is a part of grief. Later they may regret what they said or did if they can remember it. I mentioned earlier that I think some people have been angry at me for helping them stop smoking. At first they are grateful and full of appreciation, but then the grieving begins to set in, and at some point they don't know whether to be glad, sad, or mad to see me coming. They get past it after a while of course, and they are then grateful again, even if they go back to smoking.

I want to share an interesting observation with you. I have conducted stop smoking programs in small towns where I was living at the time. (I have lived in ten different states besides Canada, and different towns and cities within the states.) In those towns I was viewed as a friend and benefactor by those who stopped smoking. They would wave and go out of their way to say hello and chat awhile. Then one day as I am walking down the street, I saw one of the persons who had stopped smoking in my program. He saw me and quickly darted into a store. Aha! I knew he had gone back to smoking.

I decided not to let him get away with that, so I quickly ran into the store, found him, stuck out my hand with a grin, and let him know that I understood and that I loved him

---

**But they say anger is a good sign. It means that the person is accepting the reality.**

---

and didn't condemn him. After he got over his embarrassment, he was soooo relieved.

The last thing any person who is struggling with personal setback needs is condemnation. Bad habits are hard to break, and good habits are hard to make. But we can have a lot more success with encouragement.

Anger causes some to take up a vendetta against the cigarette industry or lash out at those around them who are still smoking, rather than sympathetically remembering how long it took themselves to stop smoking.

It's wise not to give in to anger, for anger is like a muscle. The more it is exercised, the stronger it becomes. And rage is usually followed by exhaustion and more depression, which may take the ex-smoker back to smoking again.

# Guilt

It's strange how people feel guilty over the death of someone close to them, but most do. They think back to how they might have done something differently in driving, in eating, in calling the doctor, or in reading the signs of illness. They feel guilty because they are still alive and the other person is not, and they believe that they might have prevented it if only they had...

It doesn't work quite the same for the smoker. If they sense guilt at all, it is over their having indulged their poisonous habit to the injury of their children and sometimes their marriage or for having wasted so much of their life and money. Sometimes they feel a little guilty for being angry at not being able to smoke or over the fact that they are grieving when they ought to feel liberated. Well, they do feel liberated, but there is this nagging feeling or a whole bunch of feelings that they are missing something very important that keeps diminishing their sense of freedom, that no one else can quite understand unless they have gone through it themselves. They may even feel guilty for missing cigarettes.

There is plenty to feel conflicted and guilty about, but this is no time to wallow in guilt. It is time to confess your guilt, put it behind you, and enjoy the great sense of relief. You are forgiven. You are no longer smoking, and you are looking forward to the day when you will have no desire to smoke. And then lastly, we will address accepting reality.

## Accepting Reality

Grieving doesn't end at the funeral service or the day you quit smoking. It only begins. There is often a zenith of grief and sadness at three months, six months, and again at one year, and then again at two years, but gradually the longing, the pining, the yearning, the unexplainable desire to recapture all that smoking brought you can go away or diminish enough that the ex-smoker can live with it.

If you wish to determine if you are suffering from grief from giving up smoking, answer the questions in Your Personal Grief Inventory in appendix A.

I wish I could tell you that you are now a non-smoker, but you will never be a non-smoker. You will always be an ex-smoker because smoking has permanently altered your brain, your central nervous system. The nerve pathways formed in the smoking habit remain in the brain, making one vulnerable to sights, sounds, movements, and smells that trigger reaching for a cigarette.

At this point it's a fair question to ask, "How can I get to the place where I no longer want cigarettes, and where I no longer grieve over not smoking?"

\* \* \* \* \* \* \*

# Chapter 4

# Managing Grieving for a Smoke

In this chapter I will often repeat what was written earlier in case you didn't read this book in one sitting, thus reminding you of the power of psychological addiction and the elements of grief you may face when quitting. Coping with the loss of cigarettes is more like coping with a painful divorce or breakup than coping with someone's death. In the case of a breakup, the spurned woman says, "He is still out there, and I miss him. I want him." In the case of an ex-smoker, she laments, "Cigarettes are still out there, and I miss them. I want them. Others are still enjoying them. My friends are smoking, and I want to be with my friends, but if I do..." Some smokers become recluse (sequestered) at least for awhile in order to protect themselves. But then they feel lonely.

They are conflicted. "I should be glad I'm no longer smoking. But I'm not glad. I'm sad and a little mad. I'm missing out on something. I'm free of smoking, but I'm not. I still want to smoke, but I don't. It's like a bad marriage. I can't live with them, and I can't live without them."

So how do you cope? As we study the aftermath of no longer smoking, we need to look

---

## Cigarettes are still out there, and I miss them. I want them.

---

at two related topics: staying away from cigarettes and coping with the *emotional* fallout, the grief from no longer smoking. There are many tactics, strategies, and tips to help people quit smoking and to stay away from cigarettes that can be found outside this book. But little has been written about coping with the grief of no longer smoking, so that is my emphasis here.

# Recognizing Grief

The first step in managing grief is to determine if grief is really present. It is natural that a smoker will miss cigarettes after he quits smoking. He might look for a cigarette simply out of habit. He might fumble for a pack in his pocket where he kept them for so many years. He might even be a little confused simply by a change in his routine. We shouldn't expect *grief* immediately after a deliberate (cognizant) effort to quit. He is simply adjusting to his new life.

But after a few weeks or months, if he finds himself still bewildered at the absence of a smoke, if he is wishing that he could have just one and is deliberately driving by *that* store or lingering by the cigarette counter wishing he could have just one, if he is feeling a little let down, disappointed, or a little resentful at his own decision to quit, or if he is angry at those who wanted him to quit, now he is *grieving for a smoke*. And it will probably get worse.

It may sound silly to some to think of grieving over the loss of cigarettes, but not to the grieving smoker. Once he recognizes that he is in grief, the next step is to understand that grief is a natural protest to loss and to begin working his way through it. It is helpful to know the stages of grief and confront those stages in order to help himself through them successfully. His challenge at that point is not so much to stay away from smoking as it is to deal with the grief responses that can draw him back to smoking.

## When Does Grief Set In?

As mentioned earlier if smoking has been very meaningful, then anticipatory grief can begin at the thought of quitting. So much so that some refuse to think about it until sometime later.

Often a person doesn't realize just how much smoking means to him until he quits. Then a flood of feelings emerge that he was not fully expecting nor can he fully account for. There is this vague emptiness that was filled earlier by smoking, and now the emptiness leaves him feeling... yep, empty, vulnerable, "as if a part of me is missing," lonely, "as if I am missing out on the party," certainly unfulfilled.

---

**But after a few weeks or months, if he finds himself still bewildered at the absence of a smoke ... now he is grieving for a smoke.**

---

Most people who attend a group smoking cessation program have tried to quit on their own, and they know how hard quitting can be. They may not be able to articulate at the time of trying to quit anything more than, "It's tough to quit." But underlying that simplistic view is a foreboding dread of living without something that has been very important to them. After all, it has ruled their lives. The sense of losing something so important to them, of missing out on all that smoking consciously and subconsciously mediated, is grief in the making.

# Replacement

One way to cope with the loss of something is to replace it with something else, whether it's a pet, a car, a home, or a spouse. But we can't do that with cigarettes. Smoking did not replace some natural activity. Consequently, there is no natural activity to replace smoking. Smoking is an unnatural behavior that the smoker imposed on himself. It is an artificial "need" superimposed on our central nervous system, both chemical and psychological, that clamors for relief but for which there is no genuine replacement. In one sense, it is an imaginary need, because no real need exists for breathing burning leaves wrapped in paper.

I know it doesn't seem imaginary. That's because the dopamine receptors in the brain have increased in number and size, and for a little while they clamor for attention. The central nervous system has been permanently altered. But more germane to our discussion here is that the psychological component of addiction endures long after the chemical addiction is over and causes the grief to be real.

It's worth noting that nicotine tells the smoker nothing. Its absence makes the smoker feel uncomfortable, but it is their mind, their thinking, that tells them a cigarette would make them feel better. The presence of nicotine in the brain (or the absence for a smoker) creates feelings in the body, but it tells the body nothing. It is the mind that has been conditioned to interpret the feelings as a need to smoke. This conditioning is similar to the way we interpret hunger. Many people interpret pangs in the stomach to mean they are hungry, thus food is needed. But often those stomach pangs are pangs of fatigue from eating too much and too often. The abused and tired stomach is crying out for rest, but our minds interpret the pangs as hunger.

So the desire to smoke and to keep on smoking is more than nicotine. It is a habituated neuromuscular behavior. It is a memory—thousands of memories of happy times. It is a complex set of motives that has driven this addiction for hours and days and years.

A person can use nicotine gum or patches that feed the want of a stimulant. These may help some since they release a steady low-level dose of nicotine, which avoids the sharp jolt from a cigarette. But unfortunately, continuing to stoke nicotine is continuing to hold onto a piece of a bad habit. It's like trying to stop smoking by tapering, cutting down gradually on the number of cigarettes smoked per day, which only prolongs the agony. Imagine cutting off a dog's tail a little at a time so it won't

---

## It is the mind that has been conditioned to interpret the feelings as a need to smoke.

---

hurt as much. That doesn't make sense, does it? As long as a person is smoking eight cigarettes a day, he is still hooked. Patches and pills and puffers can replace nicotine, but they cannot replace what smoking means to the smoker. The only way to be free is to stop smoking completely.

There are antithetical activities that militate against smoking. One is fitness. If a person gets into a good cardiovascular fitness program, it is counterintuitive for him to keep smoking and damaging every cell in the body. So, exercise has been an effective "replacement" for some, but not for the person who doesn't want to exercise. Pursuing an interest or hobby that has come alive since stopping smoking has helped others.

# Bereavement Therapy

Everyone is different. What works for one may not work for another. In times of grief, some are helped by turning to friends and family for comfort and encouragement. Others want to be left alone.

If a person is stuck in grief she might be helped by joining a support group. But sometimes support groups wallow in the mire of their own making so that the participants become more discouraged. I am keenly aware of some weight-loss ("therapy") groups whose members spend more time talking about how and why they broke over instead of learning how to overcome. They weighed as much (or more) a year later than when they began. But they had a good time! Putting oneself under a trained therapist may be a better answer. You can conduct an Internet search for good suggestions for coping with grief. But they don't address the peculiarities of grieving for a smoke.

# Determination/Resignation

The amount of grief—searching, pining, yearning, sadness, anger—a person suffers depends a lot on how *determined* a person is to quit smoking ... *forever.* Will power follows want power. Ambivalence is a destroyer of want power. The more determined a person is to be free of the smoking habit, the more resigned a person is to never smoke again, or the more a person has *had it* with cigarettes, the less grief they will experience. "Resigned" is a good word. To be resigned is to stop resisting the idea of never smoking again and accept

---

**If a person is stuck in grief she might be helped by joining a support group.**

---

it. That may sound contradictory, but that is the conflict that goes on in one who hasn't fully decided to quit forever. He wants to quit, but he doesn't like the idea of never smoking again. Being resigned is to give up this imagined need to smoke as if it was not possible to smoke.

When no cigarettes are available, as happened in some concentration camps during World War II, people experience little or no withdrawal. As long as cigarettes are out there and available, and the smoker has not really, *really* determined to quit forever, he will suffer more of a "divorce" from cigarettes than a "death" to cigarettes.

Smokers have to decide which is worse,

suffering the consequences of smoking, which can be lethal, or suffering the emotional consequences of not smoking, which can be extremely unpleasant but hopefully temporary. Suffering is indirectly proportional to a final decision not to smoke. What does that mean? The more final the smoker's decision is not to smoke, the less he will suffer. The less final the smoker's decision is not to smoke, the more he will suffer.

Some people need a third-party authority to control them (low internal locus of control). They don't by themselves have the will power or the ability to resist the pressure of others offering them something they kind of want. But if they can say, "My doctor told me...," that external third-party authority can help diabetics, people who are obese, and smokers say no. These kinds of persons can find help by associating with others going through similar problems.

However, even the determined, dedicated ex-smoker can still miss smoking, which is understandable based on what we covered earlier. The dedicated smoker who is now a dedicated ex-smoker trying to cope with the loss of cigarettes is not to be laughed at, scorned, or belittled. Those who are able to just walk away from smoking with little or no regrets may not appreciate what others are going through.

Smoking may not have held for them the same invested meaning that it did for those who are *grieving for a smoke*.

The grieving persons may be deep-feeling individuals, or they may be persons who had important psychological needs when they began smoking. Today they might be profession-

---

## Some people need a third-party authority to control them.

---

als, mentally disciplined and honored in their field, or skillful workers with their hands, a mechanic, a builder, an artist, but for these very individuals smoking may have filled a serious need in earlier years. I have dealt with so many who were, in all truth, weeping inside and not understanding what was going on inside them that I have great empathy for them and great respect for the grief some people go through.

# Keep Fighting

On one hand the abstaining smoker is to give up, resign, surrender the will to smoke, but at the same time, he is to fight against the urge to smoke.

Once a smoker has really decided to quit

and begins his regime *and* he is actively fighting against the urge to smoke *and is winning*, he feels little grief. He feels victorious. He has reason to celebrate, at least a little. He mustn't feel too smug, or he will let down his guard. He must keep fighting.

When a person is first quitting and is adequately coached, he will be on guard against all the triggers that call for a smoke. And if he is winning, he feels very little sense of loss. In fact, he feels good about his success at dumping the smoking habit. But after he has gone without cigarettes for a time and begins to let down his guard so that he is not actively fighting against smoking, it is then that the feelings of something missing can set in, and soon he will crave that something, and his mind will naturally turn to cigarettes.

A person won't keep up the same vigil against smoking as he did when he first seriously quit. That's the law of conservation of energy at work. But it is also the atrophy of disuse, entropy, and other appropriate terms. So if he lets down his guard too soon, the would-be ex-smoker will forget all the bad things about cigarettes—the risks, the stink, the cost, the inconvenience, etc.—and why he wanted to quit in the first place. Idealization sets in quickly as he remembers how much he enjoyed smoking and the friends he used to hang out with, and, and, and. And now he really starts to miss cigarettes. Oops! He is grieving for a smoke, maybe lightly at first, but then more and more as he relaxes his vigil.

I noticed after conducting several Five-Day Plan to Stop Smoking programs that many people returned to smoking sooner than I ex-

---

## When a person is first quitting and is adequately coached, he will be on guard against all the triggers

---

pected. So I wrote 2-5-4 Smoke No More. The "5" stood for the regular Five-Day Plan with a few additions. The "5" represented five nights in a row when they were intensely kicking the habit. Support was available for each participant. Enthusiasm ran high. At the end of the five nights, they were excited with their success. "They would never smoke again. They didn't need any more meetings." But the contract required them to attend at least three of the last four if they wanted their money back.

The "4" stood for four once-a-week follow-up meetings. This was to help them keep fighting. At the time, I charged fifty dollars per person for the program. My proposition was that if the participant attended three of the last four follow-up meetings, they would get all their money back. This was a deposit-contract designed to give them the support they wouldn't think they needed later on. I asked them to deposit as much money as needed to guarantee that they would attend three of the last four in order to get their money back. Some put in one hundred dollars. When the program was over, many left their deposit as a "thank offering." Others took it as a reward to themselves, and to keep me honest, I think.

Once when I did a stop smoking program in a work place, one person said she didn't have fifty dollars. She said she didn't have twenty-five dollars. I told her that if she was still smoking, then she had money to put up a deposit contract. But her colleagues collectively told me, no, she didn't. She would bum off of them both cigarettes and money to buy more cigarettes. Sure enough! She was unsuccessful. She hadn't invested enough sacrifice into her efforts.

Watching the results of the "4" in 2-5-4 Smoke No More were most interesting. When the first night (or day) of the last four arrived, some of them were reluctant to come. They didn't think they needed any more sessions. Some came in with a chip on their shoulder. But by the end of the evening, I would hear those same ones say, "Boy! Am I glad I came. I didn't realize how much I needed this," or

"I didn't realize how much I had slacked off." That was only four days after the five days in a row! Entropy, i.e. degradation of energy, set in quickly. That meeting was a needed boost to their resolve to "not go back."

When I wrote 2-5-4 Smoke No More, the "2" stood for two preparatory sessions getting them ready to actually quit during the five

---

## She was unsuccessful. She hadn't invested enough sacrifice into her efforts.

---

intense days. On the first night of the "2," I had the participants write on a special card all the reasons why they wanted to quit smoking. Then some of them would share what they had written. If a person heard from another a good reason they hadn't thought of, they could add it to their own list. If the group was large, fifty to one hundred, I broke them into smaller groups to share.

After that exercise, I asked them to make a gain/loss inventory. I gave them another card and asked them to write everything they could think of that they expected to gain by not smoking. At first the assignment seemed a little strange to them because they had never systematically processed such thoughts. But soon they caught on, and they wrote things such as extra money, approval from their spouse and children, improved health, etc.

Next I asked them to turn the card over and write what they expected to *lose* by not smoking. I didn't ask what they would miss about smoking even though the answers might be similar. I deliberately used the term "lose." I didn't give them any examples. Some of them thought I was joking, so they wrote things like, "I will lose the foul taste in the morning," or "I will lose having to step outside to smoke." A few perceptive persons listed things that would draw them back to smoking like, "I will lose sharing a cigarette with friends, having something to do with my hands, or having something to do after dinner." It isn't so easy to think of such things while still smoking. A few months later all of them could write without hesitation a number of things they had lost.

What I did during the program to help them quit smoking became one of the secrets to helping them stay away from cigarettes and cope with their loss. The secret was to have them keep reviewing the reasons they wanted to quit smoking and what they hoped to gain by quitting. I strongly urged them to review those lists *every* morning without fail as they awoke and at set times during the day.

Good intentions atrophy rapidly if they

are not deliberately renewed, reinforced, and acted upon. Good intentions and good resolutions are like a muscle—use it or lose it. I really leaned on them to continually read their list of reasons why they wanted to stop smoking in the first place and of the things they would lose and gain. They could add to the list at any time.

I knew from experience just how quickly their good intentions and promises would

---

## "I will lose sharing a cigarette with friends, or having something to do with my hands...."

---

dwindle. That is why I included the deposit contract to keep them coming to reinforce what they wanted in their hearts, yet would fail to accomplish if they didn't exercise the steps necessary to keep them fighting.

I also discussed with them ways to reward themselves for good behavior. I suggested that they take the money they had been spending on their habit and spend it on something that would make it worth staying away from smoking just a little longer, and just a little more longer (poor grammar noted) until they had become bona fide ex-smokers.

I should add that I am not promoting 2-5-4

Smoke No More. I wrote it while I was in Canada in the early 1980s, not for profit, and I doubt the materials are available anymore. But the concepts are available for any health educator to use. Once in a while, I still do a program in the little town where I live with materials I generate on my copy machine. But I am no longer traveling to do stop smoking programs.

Ex-smokers have to realize that waves of grief may rise to a high level before they recede again—three months, six months, one year and two years. Then, depending on the nature of the loss, anniversaries and birthdays can be hurtful. If smoking was very meaningful to a person, then the sense of loss will be that much greater. To a grieving person, I would never suggest that it will be a walk in the park. It can be tough. Triggers are everywhere to call one back to smoking. And every time the per-

---

**Ex-smokers have to realize that waves of grief may rise to a high level before they recede again....now he is grieving for a smoke.**

---

son has to deny self and feel like he is missing out on something, the more he will miss the object of his affection.

During the program, I asked the participants

to tell me all the reasons they wanted to stop smoking, like to save money, to have better health, to live longer, to avoid disease, to get control of their lives, and whatever else they suggested. I wrote all of the reasons on the board for them to see. They were all good reasons. But most of them won't hold up over time if smoking really meant a lot to them. They need a higher motivation. Sometimes a smoker will give one like "to please God" or "for my children's sake," but whatever the reason is, the smoker has to place enough value in the reason to fight to push through the grief and not succumb to the bad habit of smoking ever again.

## Keep Praying

We often say with tongue in cheek, "There is no wrong way to quit smoking." And quitting is at times the easy part. The challenge is staying away from cigarettes. Some smokers have quit a hundred times. The highest motivation is a spiritual and/or an altruistic one. The most effective way to quit and not go back is to do it for God. All over the world thousands simply stop smoking or stop chewing "betel nut" (areca nut) without a formal program when they join the Seventh-day Adventist Church.

To quit smoking for God rather than for just our own sakes instantly elevates the motivation to a higher level than self. This brings into view our responsibility to others, for one of the two great commandments in the law is, "You shall love your neighbor as yourself." However, sometimes we are so self-destructive that we need to prize our neighbor *more* than ourselves. Living for God elevates our own self-worth and raises our concern for others.

Whenever I conducted a stop smoking clinic, I ended the evening with prayer, saying to the participants that we need all the help we can get. I already knew the power of prayer, but I learned from one man just how miraculously effective prayer can be.

One of the leaders in my church in Anchorage, Alaska, was a tall ex-Texas Ranger. He still slept with a six-shooter under his pillow. He was a heavy smoker when he was younger, and he had tried and tried unsuccessfully to stop smoking. One day he went for a walk along a deserted road. He had just bought a white "ten-gallon" hat. You would think he would have been walking proudly under his new hat. But he wasn't walking proudly. He was grieving, mourning terribly, not over the loss of cigarettes but over his inability to quit smoking. In anguish he prayed aloud, "Oh God, you've got to take these cigarettes away from me." He was in such agony as he prayed that he unconsciously pulled his brand new hat from his head and crushed it to his chest, then threw it into the ditch along side the road.

He walked only a few more paces when suddenly he realized he had no desire to smoke. He sensed that he was absolutely free of cigarettes. It took a few moments for that reality to settle in, but when it did he jumped into

---

## The highest motivation is a spiritual and/or an altruistic one.

---

the air and clicked his heels. He was elated. He reached for his hat to throw it into the air in regular cowboy fashion, but it wasn't there, forgetting that he had thrown it on the ground. He walked back over the road searching for his hat, but he couldn't find it. That was several years before I met him. But from that day on he said he never wanted or was tempted to smoke.

That was a miracle, and perhaps that's how God must answer the weakest of the weak. But for most of us, He prefers to build our strength, which He does by letting us exercise our own will power, assisted by His divine power which thereafter becomes a part of our own power if we truly ask and try. I don't mean to *think about* praying as if that was praying. It isn't. I mean to really pray.

God promises freedom from disease if we obey His requirements (Deut. 7:11-15). He will reinforce our every effort to live healthfully. If we do our best, He will do the rest.

I know that giving up smoking for God raises smoking to a moral level. But smoking *is* a moral matter. When men and women bring disease and premature death on themselves by selfish indulgences, leaving a widowed spouse and fatherless or motherless children, they are behaving selfishly.

They subject their children and all around them to the poisons of burning tobacco. We've all heard about the ill effects of secondhand smoke. But secondhand smoke is not the real culprit. The real culprit is side-stream. Secondhand smoke has been filtered by the filter on the cigarette and by the smoker's lungs. But side-stream comes right off the unfiltered burning end of a cigarette. People breathing side-stream are exposed to the worst a cigarette has to offer.

A smoker needs to grab onto any ethical motivation he or she can find to keep them determined. When a person quits for God or for others, it elevates the focus from one's self to others, which gives them a sense of good will that is more gratifying than simply quitting for one's own sake. Yes, I know, it brings more shame if you fail, but you are not going to fail. You are giving up smoking for God and for good. God is waiting in the wings to provide His supernatural strength to those who sincerely ask.

I know as I write how ambivalent and conflicted smokers can be when desiring to quit, fearing both the process of quitting and the prospects of living without cigarettes. But you can make it through the grieving process.

## Grief Will Pass—Usually

For the person suffering from grief, no matter which part or parts of the process, it is important to remember that for most people these feelings will pass and life will return to some form of normality. Yet it has been my observation that for many it may take months or years to really feel free of both smoking and grief. The smoker is "freed" from smoking as soon as he quits for good. But he may not be free from this strange sense of loss for many months, sometimes years to come. But in time these feelings will either pass completely or be diminished to the point where they are bearable. At times feelings of grief may flash intermittently for a moment or for a day or two and then subside. But know that they will usually not last forever.

Some emotions may seem unbearable at the time, such as delirium tremens for the person coming off alcohol or drugs, or even a bad case of twitters from no nicotine, but they too will pass. The emotional pain of grief can be difficult, very difficult, but in time the pain subsides. At such times, if the person can't get her mind on something else, then she will just have to bear it until it goes away. That may sound heartless, but it is true. Every person experiences grief at some point in life. Different people handle grief differently. The important thing is to keep moving forward.

From time to time it might be helpful to review the "stages" of grief mentioned in chapter 3 to determine where you are in the process, knowing that such experiences are normal, and to watch yourself pass through the different stages successfully.

Ex-smokers know that they will always be ex-smokers more than non-smokers, but they can be victorious ex-smokers if they set their mind and heart on better things than smoking.

* * * * * * *

# Appendix A

# **Your Personal Grief Inventory**

The following inventory is not certified for validity and reliability; nevertheless, your answers will help you determine pretty clearly if you are experiencing grief to some extent. An authentic version would jumble the questions so that the reader might not know which response was being measured.

# Shock

|  | Strongly Disagree | Moderately Disagree | Slightly Disagree | Slightly Agree | Moderately Agree | Strongly Agree |
|---|---|---|---|---|---|---|

**Before I stopped smoking:**

a. For a long time I refused to think about quitting. ☐ ☐ ☐ ☐ ☐ ☐

b. The thought of going without cigarettes was threatening. ☐ ☐ ☐ ☐ ☐ ☐

c. I almost trembled at the thought of living without cigarettes. ☐ ☐ ☐ ☐ ☐ ☐

**When I stopped smoking:**

a. I sensed a numbness, a disorientation from my routine. ☐ ☐ ☐ ☐ ☐ ☐

b. I hadn't necessarily decided to stop for good yet. ☐ ☐ ☐ ☐ ☐ ☐

c. I found it harder to concentrate. ☐ ☐ ☐ ☐ ☐ ☐

# Shock

| | | Strongly Disagree | Moderately Disagree | Slightly Disagree | Slightly Agree | Moderately Agree | Strongly Agree |
|---|---|---|---|---|---|---|---|
| d. | I didn't wish to make any other major decisions just then. | ☐ | ☐ | ☐ | ☐ | ☐ | ☐ |
| e. | I found it difficult to cope. | ☐ | ☐ | ☐ | ☐ | ☐ | ☐ |
| f. | I felt the need to suppress how much I would miss cigarettes. | ☐ | ☐ | ☐ | ☐ | ☐ | ☐ |
| g. | I felt the need to reassure myself how happy I was for my decision to stop smoking. | ☐ | ☐ | ☐ | ☐ | ☐ | ☐ |
| h. | I felt the need to avoid stressful situations. | ☐ | ☐ | ☐ | ☐ | ☐ | ☐ |

# Rumination

Do you think of cigarettes throughout the day?

___ Never

___ Occasionally

___ Frequently

___ All the time it seems

Does it seem that the need to smoke is constantly there?

___ No

___ To some degree

___ Considerably

___ Very much so

Once the thought of smoking a cigarette comes to mind, do you find it difficult to put it out of your mind?

___ No

___ A little

___ Considerably

___ Very difficult

# Searching

Do you feel an urge to go find a cigarette?

___ Never

___ Occasionally

___ Often

___ Very often

Even though you might not take one, do you find yourself reaching for or looking for a cigarette?

\_\_\_ Never

\_\_\_ Occasionally

\_\_\_ Frequently

\_\_\_ Constantly it seems

Are you aware of where you can put your hands on a cigarette anytime if you really need one?

\_\_\_ Never

\_\_\_ Sometimes

\_\_\_ Most of the time

\_\_\_ Always

Even though you may not take one, do you look for cigarettes in the drawer or cupboard or deliberately go close by the vending machine or store where you used to get your cigarettes?

\_\_\_ Never

\_\_\_ Rarely

\_\_\_ Occasionally

\_\_\_ Frequently

# Pining

Do you find yourself not just wanting a cigarette but actually yearning for a smoke?
___ No
___ A little (perhaps)
___ Quite a lot
___ Very much so

Are there times when you wish you could smoke after all?
___ No
___ A little
___ Quite a lot
___ Very much so

Is it painful to talk about going without cigarettes?
___ No
___ A little
___ Quite a lot
___ Very much so

Even though you may be glad you don't smoke, do you ever kind of sigh, wishing you could smoke at least one?
___ No
___ Sometimes
___ Quite often
___ Very frequently

# Sequestering (Periodic Isolation)

Now that you're not smoking, do you associate less with smoking friends than you used to?
___ No
___ Slightly less
___ Quite a lot less
___ Very much less

Have any of your smoking friends or associates withdrawn from you?
___ No
___ Possibly
___ Quite a few
___ Several

If so, how much do you miss them?
___ None
___ Slightly
___ Quite a bit
___ Very much

Are there enjoyable activities that you no longer do since quitting smoking?
___ No
___ Perhaps
___ Several
___ Many

If so, how much do you miss them?
___ None
___ Slightly
___ Quite a bit
___ Very much

Are there places you no longer go since not smoking?
___ No
___ Perhaps
___ Several
___ Many

If so, how much do you miss them?
___ None
___ Slightly
___ Quite a bit
___ Very much

Do you avoid certain people since no longer smoking?
___ No
___ Perhaps
___ Some
___ Several

If so, how much do you miss them?

___ None

___ Slightly

___ Quite a bit

___ Very much

# Depression

Does it seem like a part of you is missing without cigarettes?

___ No

___ Perhaps

___ Occasionally

___ Very much so

Does not being able to smoke ever leave you depressed?

___ No

___ To some degree

___ Quite a bit

___ Very much so

Do you ever crave cigarettes to the degree that it leaves you feeling discouraged?

___ No

___ To some degree

___ Quite a bit

___ Very much so

Have you ever yearned for smoking enough to cry with or without tears?

\___ No
\___ To some degree
\___ Quite a bit
\___ Very much so

Do you feel a bleakness about living without cigarettes so that you question whether it is worth it?

\___ No
\___ To some degree
\___ Quite a bit
\___ Very much so

Do you sometimes feel you would rather smoke than miss it as much as you do?

\___ No
\___ To some degree
\___ Quite a bit
\___ Very much so

Do you feel it might be better to smoke and be happy than suffer the effects of not smoking?

\___ No
\___ Perhaps
\___ Very possible
\___ Definitely

Do you feel that smoking might do you more good than harm?

___ No
___ Perhaps
___ Very possible
___ Definitely

# Anger and Resentment

Does the smoking of others irritate you?

___ No
___ A little
___ Considerably
___ Very much

Do you have any feelings of resentment toward the whole tobacco scene, the industry, the advertising, the ever-present pressure to smoke?

___ No
___ A little
___ Considerably
___ Very much

Do you ever resent cigarettes?

___ No
___ A little
___ Considerably
___ Very much

Is it aggravating that people make such a big deal over smoking?

\_\_\_ No
\_\_\_ A little
\_\_\_ Considerably
\_\_\_ Very much

Do you ever feel a deep-seated loathing toward smoking?

\_\_\_ No
\_\_\_ A little
\_\_\_ Considerably
\_\_\_ Very much

Do you ever feel angry at the whole affair?

\_\_\_ No
\_\_\_ A little
\_\_\_ Considerably
\_\_\_ Very much

# Guilt and Shame

Do you feel guilty in any way for having smoked?

\_\_\_ No
\_\_\_ A little
\_\_\_ Considerably
\_\_\_ Very much

Do you feel your smoking has bothered others?

\_\_\_ No

\_\_\_ A little

\_\_\_ Considerably

\_\_\_ Very much

Do you ever feel angry at yourself for having
smoked?

\_\_\_ No

\_\_\_ A little

\_\_\_ Considerably

\_\_\_ Very much

Do you wish you could make up for the years
you smoked?

\_\_\_ No

\_\_\_ A little

\_\_\_ Considerably

\_\_\_ Very much

Do you ever feel as if you need to apologize and
say "I'm sorry" for your smoking?

\_\_\_ No

\_\_\_ A little

\_\_\_ Considerably

\_\_\_ Very much

# Accepting Reality

Is there an emptiness about never smoking again that leaves sadness?

___ No
___ A little
___ Considerably
___ Very much

When you think of never smoking again, does a little flash of fear or panic ever pass over you?

___ Never
___ Occasionally
___ Often
___ Every time it seems

Although you may be glad that you are not smoking anymore, do you miss cigarettes?

___ No
___ A little
___ Considerably
___ Very much

Does the absence of cigarettes ever leave you feeling lonely?

___ Never
___ Occasionally
___ Often
___ Every time it seems

Do you feel you are missing out on some of life's enjoyments by not smoking?

\_\_\_ No

\_\_\_ A little

\_\_\_ Quite a lot

\_\_\_ Very much

Do you feel that you will never smoke again?

\_\_\_ No

\_\_\_ A little

\_\_\_ Quite certain

\_\_\_ Definitely

# Appendix B

# Grief Responses by Early Mappers

This section contains the findings of research by early psychologists in the area of grief recovery:

Eliot, Thomas D. "The Bereaved Family." *The Annals of the American Academy of Political and Social Science* 160 (1932): pp. 184-190.

*Immediate Effects of Bereavement*
1. Abandon
2. Refusal or rejection of the facts (including dissociation of emotion or sense of unreality)
3. Preternatural or detached pain
4. Shock, in the neurological sense
5. Exaltation
6. Self-injury
7. Repression
8. Blame of self or others, revenge

9. The intense longing of grief

"The first eight occur in various sequences and combinations with the last. Without grief (it may be assumed) the others would not arise. Ordinarily, however, the word 'grief' is used so loosely, to cover all theses phenomena, that it has little specific descriptive value" (185).

*Secondary Reactions*
1. Escape, or attempted escape from the conflict, e.g., use of drugs, moving of residence, suicide, social distractions, or illusions.
2. Defense and repression, e.g., removing all reminders, deliberate forgetting, postural self-control, or certain "mental diseases."
3. Compensation (in the narrower sense), e.g., rationalization, beliefs and cults, rituals of guilt or contrition, perpetuation of memory of deceased or of wish or supposed will of deceased, revenge, penance of "overdetermined" grief.
4. Masochism and exhibition, e.g., voluptuaries of grief, recluses, ascetics, and the like.

5. Identification (introjective), e.g., stepping into the role of the deceased or "carrying the spirit" of the deceased.
6. Transference and substitution (involving projection), e.g., reattachment of affections to new mother, child, or spouse; espousal of charities or causes.

\* \* \* \* \* \* \*

Lindeman, Erich, MD. *Beyond Grief.* New York, NY: Jason Aronson, 1979, p. 274.

Early mapping with special focus on acute grief drawn from 101 patients:
1. Somatic distress, waves of
    a. Tightness of throat
    b. Shortness of breath
    c. Need for sighing
    d. Empty feeling in the abdomen
    e. Lack of muscular power
    f. An intense subjection distress described as tension or mental pain—Therefore to avoid precipitation of this reaction the bereaved would "deliberately keep from thought all references to the deceased" (p. 61).
2. Altered sensorium

   a. Slight sense of reality
   b. Increased emotional distance from other people
   c. Preoccupation with the image of the deceased
3. Feelings of guilt
4. Disconcerting loss of warmth toward others
   a. Irritability
   b. Anger—hostility
   c. Stiff social interaction
5. Change of activity not retardation
   a. Push of speech especially of the deceased
   b. Restlessness
   c. Moving about in an aimless fashion
   d. Continual searching
   e. Routines of past are uninteresting and require effort, especially regarding the deceased

* * * * * * *

Engel, George, L. "Grief and Grieving." *American Journal of Nursing* 64 (1964): pp. 93-98.
1. Shock and Disbelief
   a. Refusal to accept or comprehend the fact

    b. Stunned, numb feeling

    c. Refusal to overtly acknowledge reality of the death

    d. Intellectual acceptance

    e. Emotional suppression of pain of loss, muted occasional flashes of despair and anguish

2. Developing Awareness

    a. Accepts consciousness of anguish of loss

    b. Anger at others, at self

    c. Crying with anguish and despair at zenith or inwardly

    d. Ambivalence toward deceased affects degree

3. Restitution or mourning

    a. Often ritualized and institutionalized

    b. Personal beliefs mold

4. Resolving the Loss

    a. A void is felt, defeat in sense of intactness, wholeness of the self

    b. Awareness of own body

    c. Preoccupation with the loss, then the person, then person idealized

5. Idealization

    a. Repression of all negative and hostile feelings toward deceased

    b. Produces guilt, remorse, fear

c.  Distinct [eclectic] image formed of the deceased
d.  Identification via adopting admired traits of the deceased
e.  Psychic dependence diminishes
f.  Sadness, yearning diminish
g.  Interest turn to other persons and matters

* * * * * * *

Parkes, Colin Murray. "Components of the Reaction to Loss of Limb, Spouse or Home." *Journal of Psychosomatic Research* 16 (1972): pp. 343-349.

The seven major aspects of many bereavement reactions:
1.  Process of realization from denial or avoidance of recognition of the loss toward acceptance
2.  An alarm reaction; anxiety, restlessness, and the physiological accompaniments of fear
3.  Urge to search
4.  Anger and guilt
5.  Feelings of internal loss of self or mutilation

6. Identification phenomenon; adoption of traits, mannerisms, or symptoms of the lost person
7. Pathological variants of grief; excessive, prolonged, inhibited [delayed] distorted form

\* \* \* \* \* \* \*

Ramsay, Ronald W. and Renee Noorbergen. *Living With Loss*. New York, NY: Wm. Morrow & Co. Inc., 1981, p. 214.

1. Shock
2. Disorganization
3. Searching behavior
4. Emotional components
   a. Desolate pining
   b. Despair
   c. Guilt anxiety
   d. Jealousy
   e. Shame
   f. Protect, aggression
5. Letting go
6. Resolution and acceptance
7. Reintegration

\* \* \* \* \* \* \*

Glick, Ira O., Robert S. Weiss, and C. Murray Parkes. *The First Year of Bereavement.* New York, NY: John Wiley & Sons, Inc., 1974, pp. 119-127.

1. Ceremonies of leave-taking; ritualized
2. Grieving
    a. Pervasive sadness (p. 119)
    b. Sleeplessness
    c. Deeper depression
    d. Daily reality of their loss lasted weeks to months; two months had passed zenith
3. Indications of grief
    a. Somber clothing
    b. Sequestering (isolation) withdrawal from social life (pp. 120-122)
4. Obsessional review of the search for meaning [preoccupation]
    a. Dwelt on topic in conversation, self (p. 126) [talked about not smoking]
    b. Reproach, "If I had then..."
    c. Search for the why
5. Solitary mourning; concern for their own sanity

Note: Glick does not "map" but employs the same terminology; shock, disbelief, anger, guilt, despair, cold [numb] without emotion, anguished sobbing, physical distress, bewilderment, fear of being unable to manage.

\* \* \* \* \* \* \*

Westberg, Granger E. *Good Grief.* Minneapolis, MN: Fortress Press, 1962, pp 1-64.
1. State of shock
   a. Stunned
   b. Temporary escape from reality
2. Expression of emotion; awareness of dreadful loss
3. Feel depressed and lonely; utter depression and lonely
4. Physical symptoms of distress (not from acute as Lindeman)
5. Panic from own inability to stop preoccupation with the deceased
6. Guilt
7. Anger and resentment
8. Resist returning to normality
9. Hope gradually comes through
10. Reality affirmed

\* \* \* \* \* \* \*

Kubler-Ross, Elisabeth. *On Death and Dying.* New York, NY: Routledge, 1969.

1. Denial and isolation
2. Anger
3. Bargaining
4. Acceptance
5. Hope

* * * * * * *

Peretz, David. *Loss and Grief; Psychological Management in Medical Practice.* Edited by Bernard Schoenberg. New York, NY: Columbia University Press, 1970, pp. 22-24.

1. Shock and numbness
2. Bewilderment and weeping
3. Continually returning thoughts yields fear of losing emotional control
4. Physical reactions
   a. Deep sighing
   b. Weakness
   c. Anxiety, tension, sexual desire decreased
5. Denial, may refuse to talk about it because of pain
6. Painful yearning and loneliness for the lost object

    a.  Weep tearlessly

    b.  Sense of emptiness

7.  Feelings of unreality; illusory phenomena

8.  Guilt

9.  Irrational anger

\* \* \* \* \* \* \*

Wylie, Betty Jane. *Beginnings, A Book for Widows*. Toronto, Canada: McClellan & Stewart, 1977.

1.  Shock

    a.  Initial shock

    b.  Emotional release

    c.  Loneliness

2.  Denial

    a.  Depression

    b.  Panic

    c.  Hostility

    d.  Guilt

    e.  Inability to return to normal activity

3.  Acceptance

    a.  Gradual hope

    b.  Struggle to affirm reality

\* \* \* \* \* \* \*

# Appendix C

# **Additional Resources**

The following books and scientific articles contributed to the concepts included in this book. I am and you are, if you read this book, indebted to the vast amount of research and discussions made by the authors.

Bejerot, Nils, MD. "A Theory of Addiction as an Artificially Induced Drug." American Journal of Psychiatry 128, no. 7 (January 1972): pp. 842-846.

Bellwood, Lester K., ThD, PhD. "Grief Work in Alcoholism Treatment." Alcohol Health and Research World 1975: pp. 8-11.

Bern, Daryl J. Beliefs, Attitudes and Human Affairs. Belmont, CA: Brooks/Cole Publishing Co., Div. of Wadsworth Publishers, 1970: p. 114.

Bogdan, Robert, and Steven J. Taylor. Introduction to Qualitative Research Methods. Toronto,

Canada: John Wiley & Sons, Inc., 1975: p. 266.

Bollinger, C. T., and K. O. Fargerstrom, editors. The Tobacco Epidemic. Basel, Switzerland: S. Karger, 1997.

Bonanno, George A. The Other Side of Sadness. New York, NY: Basic Books Inc., 2009.

Bowlby, John. Attachment and Loss; Anxiety and Loss. Vol. 1, Attachment, 1969; Vol. 2, Separation, 1973. New York, NY: Basic Books Inc.

———. "Processes of Mourning." International Journal of Psycho-Analysis 42, no. 45 (1961): pp. 317-340.

Bozzetti, L. P. "Group Psychotherapy with Addicted Smokers." Psychoher Psychasom 20 (1972): pp. 172-175.

Bugen, Larry A. "Human Grief: A Model for Prediction and Intervention." American Journal of Ortho Psychiatry 47, no. 2 (April 1977): pp. 196-206.

Caplan, Gerald, and Marie Killilee. Support Systems and Mutual Help. New York, NY: Grune & Stratton, 1976: p. 325.

Caplan, L. M., and T. P. Hackett. "Emotional Effects of Lower and Limb Amputation in the Aged." New England Journal of Medicine 269 (1963): p. 1166f.

Christen, Arden G., DDS, and Kenneth H. Cooper, MD. "Strategic Withdrawal From Cigarette Smoking." CA-A Cancer Journal for Clinicians 29, no. 2 (March-April 1979): pp. 96-107.

Clayton, Paula, et. al. "A Study of Normal

Bereavement." American Journal of Psychiatry 125, no. 2 (August 1968): pp. 168-178.

Colletti, Gep, and Steven A. Kopel. "Maintaining Behavior Change: An Investigation of Three Maintenance Strategies and the Relationship of Self-Attribution to the Long-Term Reduction of Cigarette Smoking." Journal of Consulting and Clinical Psychology 47, no. 3 (1979): pp. 614-617.

Dunn, William L. Jr. Smoking Behaviour: Motives and Incentives. Toronto, Canada: John Wiley & Sons, Inc., 1973: p. 308.

Dzegede, Sylvi A., MA, John R. Hackworth, PhD, and Steven W. Pike, MA. "Factors That Differentiate Smokers From Ex-smokers In A Florida Metropolitan Area." Public Health Reports 96, no. 4 (June-August 1981): pp. 326-334.

Eisinger, Richard A. "Nicotine and Addiction to Cigarettes." British Journal Addiction 66 (1971): pp. 150-156.

———. "Psychosocial Predictors of Smoking Behavior Change." Social Science & Medicine 6 (1972): pp. 137-144.

———. "Psychosocial Predictors of Smoking Recidivism." Journal of Health & Social Behavior 12 (December 1971): pp. 355-362.

Eliot, Thomas D. "The Bereaved Family." The Annals of the American Academy of Political and Social Science 160 (March 1932): pp. 184-190.

Engel, George L. "Grief & Grieving." American

Journal of Nursing 64 (1964) pp. 93-98.

Fishbein, Martin, and Icek Ajzen. Belief, Attitude, Intention & Behaviour. Philippines: Addison-Wesley Publishing Company, 1975: p. 877.

Freedman, Morris. "Notes on Grief in Literature" in Schoenberg, et. al., Loss & Grief: Psychological Management in Medical Practice. New York, NY: Columbia University Press, 1970: pp. 339-346.

Fried, M. Grieving for a Lost Home. Edited by Leonard Duhl. New York, NY: Basic Books, 1962.

Friedson, Eliot. Profession of Medicine. New York, NY: Dodd Mead & Co., 1920.

Glaser, Barney G., and Angelin L. Strauss. The Discovery of Grounded Theory. Chicago, IL: Aldine Atherton, 1967: p. 277.

Glick, Ira O., Robert S. Weiss, and C. Murray Parker. The First Year of Bereavement. New York: NY: John Wiley & Sons, Inc., 1974: p. 311.

Gorden, Raymond L. Unidimensional Sealing of Social Variables. New York, NY: The Free Press, 1977: p. 175.

Gritz, Ellen R. Smoking Behavior and Tobacco Use: Advances in Substance Abuse. Edited by Nancy K. Mello. Stamford, CT: Jai Press, Inc., 1980: pp. 91-158.

Hamilton, Scott B., and Philip H. Bornstein. "Broad Spectrum Behavioral Approach to Smoking Cessation: Effects of Social Support and Paraprofessional Training on the Maintenance of Treatment Effects." Journal of Consulting

& Clinical Psychology, American Psychological Association, Inc. 47, no. 3 (1979): pp. 598-600.

Harrup, Temple. "Addictive Processes in Tobacco." Quoted in "Progress in Smoking Cessation." *Proceedings of International Conference on Smoking Cessation.* American Cancer Society, U.S. Department of Health and Human Services (1979): p. 241.

Harrup, Temple, Bruce A. Hansen, and Krikar Soghikian, MD, MPH. "Clinical Methods in Smoking Cessation: Description and Evaluation of a Stop Smoking Clinic." American Journal of Public Health 69, no. 12 (December 1979).

Hunt, William A., and Joseph D. Matarazzo. "Three Years Later: Recent Developments in the Experimental Modification of Smoking Behavior." Journal of Abnormal Psychology 81, no. 2 (1973): pp. 107-114.

Issac, Stephen, and William B. Michael. Handbook in Research & Evaluation. San Diego, CA: Edits Publisher, 1971: pp. 186.

Jackson, Edgar N. The Many Faces of Grief. Nashville, TN: Parthenon Press, 1972-1977.

Jaffe, J. H., L. S. Goodman, and A. Gilman. Drug Addiction and Drug Abuse in the Pharmacological Basis of Therapeutics. 5th ed. New York, NY: MacMillan, 1975: pp. 284-324.

Jaffe, J. H., M. E. Jarvik, M. A. Lipton, A. DiMacio, and K. F. Killam. Tobacco Use and Tobacco Use Disorder in Psychopharmacology: A Generation of Progress. New York, NY: Raven Press, 1978: pp. 1665-1676.

Johnson, Vernon E. I'll Quit Tomorrow. Revised ed. San Francisco, CA: Harper & Row, 1980: p. 182.

Kaufman, Edward, MD. "A Psychiatrist Views an Addict Self-Help Program." American Journal of Psychiatry 128, no. 7 (January 1972): pp. 846-852.

Kirscht, John P. "Perceptions of Control and Health Beliefs." Canadian Journal of Behavioral Science 4, no. 3 (1972): pp. 225-237.

Kumar, R., and M. Lader. "Nicotine and Smoking." Spectrum Publishers 6 (1981): pp. 127-164.

Lagerspetz, Kari Y.H. "Comparative Psychopharmacology: Current Developments in Psychopharmacology." Spectrum Publishers 6 (1981).

Li, Peter. Social Research Methods: An Introduction. Toronto, Canada: Butterworths, 1981: p. 150.

Lindemann, Erich, MD. Beyond Grief. New York, NY: Jason Aronson, 1979: p. 274.

Lindzey, Gardner, ed. Assessment of Human Motives. Toronto, Canada: Holt, Rinehart & Winston, 1958: p. 273.

Mackeown, Thomas. The Role of Medicine, Dream Mirage or Nemeses. London, England: The Nuffield Provincial Hospital Trust, 1976.

Mahoney, Michael J. "Research Issues in Self-Management." Journal of Behavior Therapy 3 (1972): pp. 45-63.

Mico, Paul R., and Helen S. Ross. Health Education and Behavioral Science. Oakland, CA: Third Party Associates, Inc., 1975: p. 207.

Mullen, Patricia Dolan, PH, and Richard Reynolds, PH. "The Potential of Grounded Theory for Health Education, Research: Linking Theory & Practice." Health Education Monographs 6, no. 3 (fall 1978): pp. 280-294.

Murray, Edward J. Motivation and Emotion. Englewood Cliffs, NJ: Prentice Hall Inc., 1964: p. 118.

McCatty, Cressy, AM. "Patterns of Learning Projects Among Professional Men." Ontario Institute for Studies in Education (1973): p. 134.

McFall, Richard M. "Smoking-Cessation Research." Journal of Consulting and Clinical Psychology 46, no. 4 (1978): pp. 703-712.

Oppenheim, A. N. Questionnaire Design and Attitude Measurement. New York, NY: Basic Books Inc., 1966: p. 298.

Parkes, Colin Murray. Bereavement Studies of Grief in Adult Life. London, England: Tavistock Publications, 1972: p. 233.

———. "Components of the Reaction to Loss of a Limb, Spouse, or Home." Journal of Psychosomatic Research 16 (1972): pp. 343-349.

———. "Psycho-Social Transitions: A Field for Study." Social Science & Medicine 5 (1971): pp. 101-115.

———. "Psycho-Social Transitions: Comparisons Between Reactions to Loss of Limb and Loss of a Spouse." British Journal of Psychiatry (1975): pp. 204-210.

———. "'Seeking' and 'Finding' A Lost Object:

Evidence from Recent Studies of the Reaction to Bereavement." Social Science & Medicine 4 (1970): pp. 187-201.

Paxton, Roger. "The Effects of a Deposit Contract As A Component In A Behavioral Program For Stopping Smoking." Behavioral Research and Therapy 18 (1980): pp. 45-50.

Peele, Stanton. "The Addiction Experience." Addictions 24, no. 2 (1977).

Peretz, David. "Development and Loss, & Reaction to Loss." 2nd article. Loss & Grief: Psychological Management in Medical Practice. New York, NY: Columbia University Press, 1970.

Pertschuk, Micael J., Ovide F. Pomerleau, David Adkins, and Celia Hirsh. "Smoking Cessation: The Psychological Costs." Addictive Behaviors Center for Behavioral Medicine, University of Pennsylvania 4 (1979): pp. 345-348.

Ramsay, Ronald W., and Rene Noorbergen. Living With Loss. New York, NY: William Morrow & Co. Inc., 1981: p. 214.

Reeder, Leo G. Handbook of Scales and Indicies of Health Behavior. Pacific Palisades, CA: Goodyear Publishing Co., Inc., 1976: p. 540.

Richard, Elaine, and Ann C. Shepard. "Giving Up Smoking: A Lesson In Loss Theory." American Journal of Nursing (April 1981): pp. 755-757.

Rokeach, Milton. The Nature of Human Values. New York, NY: The Free Press, 1973: p. 438.

Sanders, Catherine M. "Comparison of Younger and Older Spouses in Bereavement Outcome." Omega 11, no. 3 (1980-1981): pp. 217-233.

Sanders, Catherine M. A Manual for the Grief Experience Inventory. Washington D.C: Consulting Psychologists Press, 1979.

Sarbin, Theodore R., and Larry P. Nucci. "Self-Reconstitution Process: A Proposal for Reorganizing The Conduct of Confirmed Smokers." Journal of Abnormal Psychology 81, no. 2 (1973): pp. 182-195.

Schlegel, Ronald, and Melodie Kasnetsky. "Preventive Medicine." Academic Press Inc. 6 (1977): pp. 454-461.

Schoenberg, Bernard, ed., Arthur Carr, David Peretz, and Austin Kutscher. Loss and Grief: Psychological Management in Medical Practice. New York, NY: Columbia University Press, 1970.

Schroeder, Elaine, and Joanne E. Hall, ed. The Birth of a Defective Child: A Cause for Grieving. Toronto, Canada: J.B Lippincott, 1974: p. 159, 264.

Schulz, Richard. The Psychology of Death, Dying and Bereavement. Reading, MA: Addison-Wesley Publishing Co., 1978: p. 187.

Schwartz, Jerome L., PH. "Review & Evaluation of Methods of Smoking Cessation – Summary of a Monograph." Public Health Reports 94, no. 6 (November-December 1979): pp. 558-563.

Simpson, Michael A. The Facts of Death. New Jersey: Prentice Hall Inc., 1979: p. 276.

Singh, Jasbir M., Lyle Miller, and Lal Harbans. Drug Addiction. New York, NY: Futura Pub. Co. Inc., 1972: p. 397.

Solomon, Richard L., and John D. Corbit. "An Opponent-Process Theory of Motivation: Cigarette Addiction." Journal of Abnormal Psychology 81, no. 2 (1973): pp. 158-171.

Speck, Peter, MA, BSc. Loss and Grief in Medicine. London, England: Bailliere Tindall, 1978: p. 175.

Stepney, R. "Smoking Behaviour: A Psychology of the Cigarette Habit." British Journal of Diseases of the Chest 74, no. 325 (1980): pp. 325-344.

Tamerin, John S., MD, and Charles P. Neumann. "Casualties of the Antismoking Campaign." Comprehensive Psychiatry 14, no. 1 (January-February 1973): pp. 35-40.

Tamerin, John S., MD. "The Psychodynamics of Quitting Smoking in a Group." American Journal of Psychiatry 1291, no. 5 (November 1972): pp. 589-595.

Thornton, Raymond E., ed. Smoking Behavior: Physiological and Psychological Influences. London and New York: Churchill Livingston, 1978: p. 405.

Tompkins, Eilvan S., PhD. "Psychological Model for Smoking Behaviour." American Journal of Public Health 56, no. 12 (December 1966): pp. 17-20.

Turner, R. Jay. "Social Support as a Contingency in Psychological Well-Being." Journal of Health and
Social Behavior 22 (December 1981): pp. 357-367.

Vachon, Mary L. S. "Grief & Bereavement Following

the Death of a Spouse." Canadian Journal of Psychiatry 21 (1976): pp. 35-43.

————. "Predictors and Correlates of High Distress in Adaptation to Conjugal Bereavement." American Journal of Psychiatry (1981 or 1982).

————. "Type of Death As A Determinant In Acute Grief" in Acute Grief: Counseling the Bereaved. Columbia University Press, 1981: pp. 14-22.

*Webster's New Collegiate Dictionary.* Springfield, MA: Merriam-Webster G. & C. Merriam Company, 1973.

Weiss, Carol H., Evaluation Research. New Jersey: Prentice Hall Inc., 1972: p. 159.

Weiss, Robert S. Loneliness–The Experience of Emotional and Social Isolation. Cambridge, MA: Massachusetts Institute of Technology, 1973.

Werner-Beland, Jean A. "Grief in Parents of a Child With a Birth Handicap." Chapter 5. Grief Responses to Long-Term Illness and Disability. Reston, VA: Prentice Hall Co., 1980: p. 219.

Westberg, Granger E. Good Grief. Minneapolis, MN: Fortress Press, 1971: p. 64.

World Health Organization Expert Committee. "Smoking and Its Effect on Health." WHO Technical Report Series #568 (1975): pp. 7–73.

Williams, D. G. "Different Cigarette-Smoker Classification Factors & Subjective State in Acute Abstinence." Psychopharmacology 64 (February 22, 1979): pp. 231-235.

Wolinsky, Frederic D. The Sociology of Health. Toronto, Canada: Little Brown & Co., 1980.

Wylie, Betty Jane. Beginnings: A Book for Widows. Toronto, Canada: McClelland & Stewart, 1977.

Zuzich, Ann M. "Grief in Parents of a Child With A Birth Handicap." Chapter 5. Grief Responses to Long-Term Illness and Disability. Reston, VA: Prentice Hall Co., 1980: p. 219.

\* \* \* \* \* \* \* \*

We invite you to view the complete
selection of titles we publish at:

**www.TEACHServices.com**

Please write or email us your praises, reactions, or
thoughts about this or any other book we publish at:

# TEACH Services, Inc.
P U B L I S H I N G
## *www.TEACHServices.com*

P.O. Box 954
Ringgold, GA 30736

**info@TEACHServices.com**

TEACH Services, Inc., titles may be purchased in bulk for
educational, business, fund-raising, or sales promotional use.
For information, please e-mail:

**BulkSales@TEACHServices.com**

Finally, if you are interested in seeing
your own book in print, please contact us at

**publishing@TEACHServices.com**

We would be happy to review your manuscript for free.

www.ingramcontent.com/pod-product-compliance
Lightning Source LLC
Chambersburg PA
CBHW060542100426
42742CB00013B/2419